Choice Menu For Mother's Day (TAKE IT OR LEAVE IT)
~~~~~~ ~~~~~~ ~~~~~~~~

Special Guests: Maw Broon & Auntie Catherine

*****Five Courses*****

To start, as a pair o' teeth   *that's 'APERITIF'!*

Fresh Fruit Smoothie

and if Auntie Catherine's bus isnae late

**Soup o' the Day - Lentil and Bacon Broth wi' Bread Rolls and
Raspberry Jam**

Main Course o' the Day

Fish Cakes and Cheesy Beans on Toast

Afters

Baked Rice Pudding wi' Raspberry Jam

After Afters

Pancakes, Raisin Scones and mair Jam

After After Afters

**Peppermint Creams, Marzipan Sweeties,
Walnut Tablet and Shortbread**

Your waiters today: Horace, Ane and Ither Twin

Table Layin': Bairn

Washin' up Rota: Horace (cos he can reach the sink)

Dryin' Rota: Twins

Tablecloth put awayer and sweeper upper, and hooverin': Bairn

Doggie Bag for Auntie Catherine: Horace

Service not included

5 COURSES? JINGS!

THAT'S MAIR THAN ST ANDREWS!

No, it's no' — they've got 11.

MAW BROON'S
Cooking with Bairns

MAW BROON'S
Cooking
with
Bairns

That's us!

with Catherine Brown

WAVERLEY
BOOKS

Published 2010 by Waverley Books Ltd., 144 Port Dundas Road, Glasgow, Scotland, G4 0HZ.

Recipes and 'How to...' text © 2010 Catherine Brown.

Catherine Brown has asserted her right under the Copyright, Designs and Patents Act, 1988, to be identified as the author of the recipes, 'How to...' text and historical information on Scottish food. www.foodinscotland.co.uk

Broons text © 2010 D.C. Thomson & Co., Ltd.

The Broons logo and **The Broons** characters appear courtesy of
D.C. Thomson & Co., Ltd. and are © 2010 D.C. Thomson & Co., Ltd.

The Broons text is by David Donaldson, **The Broons** scriptwriter,
with additional material by Waverley Books Ltd.

Cover and endpaper illustrations are by Peter Davidson
© 2010 D.C. Thomson & Co., Ltd.

'How to...' text illustrations © 2010 Waverley Books Ltd.
Other line artwork by Hugo Breingan © 2010 Waverley Books Ltd.

The publishers gratefully acknowledge Scottish Language Dictionaries for permission to reproduce
J.K. Annand's poem 'Mince and Tatties' and Mr Adam McNaughtan for permission to reproduce
his 'Jeely Piece Song' ('Skyscraper Wean').

All the recipes in this book have been thoroughly tested, and, we hope, explained in the simplest possible way.
The author and publishers are grateful for the assistance of the following young mothers in Arran:
Esther Brown, Judi Worthington, Vivien Crichton and Annelies Slaats.

The publishers would welcome comments and observations.
Please e-mail us at **cookingwithbairns@waverley-books.co.uk**

A catalogue record for this book is available from the British Library.

ISBN: 978-1-902407-99-9

Printed and bound in Scotland by D.C. Thomson & Co., Ltd.,
West Ward Works, Guthrie Street, Dundee DD1 5BR.

Afore ye start! A word fae me.

The thing about us Broons that's a bit unusual is that there's that many o' us! I sometimes think I've got a hoose fu' o' bairns. I've been too guid tae the bigger anes ower the years — Hen, Joe, Maggie an' Daphne, no' tae mention Paw an' Granpaw! I've aye put their tea on the table. I wish they'd learned tae cook when they were wee!

I was chattin' tae Auntie Catherine and she was sayin' the same — that I should mak' sure that Horace, the Twins and the Bairn learn aboot proper cookin'. She says there are lots o' youngsters that just need a wee bit help. So we've made this book for you all — a proper cookin' book to get you on yer way. Ye can hae a lot o' fun in the kitchen, and learn how tae cook at the same time!

We first met Auntie Catherine up at Mallaig on oor holidays — afore we had the But an' Ben. Whit bonnie! It was oor Hen that got me chattin' wi' Catherine. She'd been watchin' him causin' a bit o' a stir wi' the clam divers. He's that tall that he disnae need the mask, snorkel and flippers like the ithers — he just goes dookin' for clams, just like for aipples!

After we'd had a good laugh, we blethered aboot this an' that and got quite pally — and we still are! We kept in touch — an' that's how she became oor Auntie Catherine! She's a dab hand at the cookin'! We're that proud when we see her writin' in the papers aboot food. We've got a' her books at No 10.

So — you'll want to get into the kitchen and start cookin'. We've done everything we can to help you wi' the tricky bits, an' there's pictures for every step to make things really clear.

There's bound tae be times, though, when something burns or disnae turn oot the way you'd expected. Dinna gie up. Making a mistake may not taste so good but it's one of the best ways to learn. A' the best cooks make mistakes. Just have another go.

These recipes are simple anes for making real food. And once ye get the hang o' the basics, ye'll probably hae my lot roond chappin' the door wantin' their tea! They can smell a guid aipple pie fae a mile awa'!

— Maw

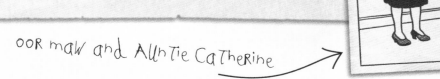

OOR maw and AuhTie CaTheRine →

Start Easy
– Get Shopping

When you choose something to cook, start with something easy – that way you begin at the beginning by mastering the basic skills.

You'll see that Maw and I have not used too many of the ready-made products that food manufacturers have invented to take the time and effort – and skill – out of cooking. When you use these off-the-shelf things you don't learn the basic cooking skills. If you buy vegetables that are already chopped, or a packet of custard powder that just needs boiling water added, you don't learn how to chop vegetables or how to thicken a sauce without getting it all lumpy. Besides, the food manufacturer will always charge you more for these convenience foods just as they will charge you even more for ready-made meals. Ready-made meals are all about *not* cooking and *not* knowing what's going into your food. Have a good read at what's written on the packaging for these convenience foods – often there is a long list of things that have been added including chemical colourings, preservatives and suchlike.

Most of the time Maw and I like to start cooking from scratch so we know what's going into our food. Fish suppers from the chippie are okay because that's basically just fish and potatoes but some of the things that go into ready-made meals don't sound good at all to me. Choosing good, fresh ingredients is just as important as learning to cook. Don't be afraid to talk to a butcher or a fishmonger, whether at your local shop or supermarket counter. They are the people who know most about what they're selling and you can ask about things you don't know.

Another important thing to remember when you're shopping is that some foods are more readily available at certain times of the year and will be cheaper and of a better quality during that season. Strawberries from Spain in December might be tempting but they will never taste as good as Scottish strawberries in summer. Ingredients that have travelled for many hundreds of miles by road or air will be a lot dearer and they are not helping the environment.

When you decide what you want to cook, the first thing to do is to go shopping for the best ingredients!

Auntie Catherine

Kitchen Rules

BEFORE COOKING

- wash hands
- put on apron
- read the recipe carefully
- gather equipment
- preheat oven
- collect ingredients
- weigh and measure out the quantities

WHILE COOKING

- do not leave frying pans or fryers on the heat if you have to leave the kitchen
- turn all handles of pots inward so they don't get knocked off the cooker
- set a timer to remind you of the baking or cooking time.
- be very careful when using a sharp knife

WHEN YOU HAVE TIME

- wash up dishes
- tidy up in the kitchen
- set table

Hey, This egg is bad!
Don't blame me, I only laid The Table!

A few words fae me aboot fussy eaters!

Some bairns can cause a richt stushie at teatime. You widna believe it but my twa strappin' boys Hen and Joe used tae mak' a big fuss aboot eatin' their porridge. They love it noo! A wee bit of persistence and a spot o' raspberry jam did the trick (a wee tip fae ma mither-in-law).

Wi' bairns ye've sometimes got tae be a wee bit clever and a wee bit patient (and a wee bit sneaky) aboot getting them tae eat whit's guid for them! Getting them interested in cookin' is a great way to get them interested in eatin' of course.

Bairns can be scared o' new foods they havnae tried afore. Dinna mak' a big fuss but try to get them to try a tiny wee bit. Be firm but dinna ever shout and dinna force bairns tae eat things they really dinna like. If they are brave enough to eat the new thing, give them a big cuddle. Bairns like cuddles. Maws too! An' try tae mak' meal times relaxed times. A' the family should sit thegither at the table. Bairns can eat whit you are eatin' so dinna encourage separate dinners. Maws are far too busy for that carry on!

In the meantime though, bairns need their vitamins. So ye need to be a wee bit canny. If they cannae see the vegetables, they'll maybe no ken they're there. Chop them intae wee totie pieces and 'hide' them in your stews, mashed tatties, croquettes or fish cakes. Purée vegetables in soups and sauces and call it 'colouring'. If fruit's a problem, try fruit juices — they still hae a' the same vitamins — and stewed fruit or fruit purée wi' ice cream is braw! Or be clever. Turn it intae a game: 'How many colours o' fruit an' vegetables can we eat every day? I know you can sing a rainbow, but can you eat a rainbow?'

Nutrition can be confuddling but ye dinna need to get yersel' in a fankle aboot it. Horace has written a simple guide for ye (see pages 12–13) and my rule is: if you hae a balanced diet every day — a wee bit o' everything an' no too much o' onything — then ye dinna need fancy vitamin pills and ye can treat yersel' to the occasional cake, crisp or sweetie withoot puttin' on the beef. Oh and dinna cook wi' ower much salt or sugar. Start them young and they might no' get the taste for ower sweet or salty things.

Well I've blethered on long enough aboot eatin', let's go an' talk to Auntie Catherine and get to the fun part — the cookin'!

Maw x

A WORD FAe THe TWiNS: CHIPS!!!!!!!!!!!!!!

Handy Kitchen Tools

Large pot with lid

Pie dish

Girdle

Scissors

Medium saucepan with lid

23 cm × 33 cm baking tray

Rolling pin

Measuring jug

Small saucepan without lid

18 cm × 25 cm baking tray

Small sieve

Digital scales

Frying pan

22 cm cake sandwich tins × 2

Large sieve

Timer

Casserole

25 cm large cake tin

Grater

Chopping board

How do you know when an elephant has been in your fridge?
Footprints in the butter!

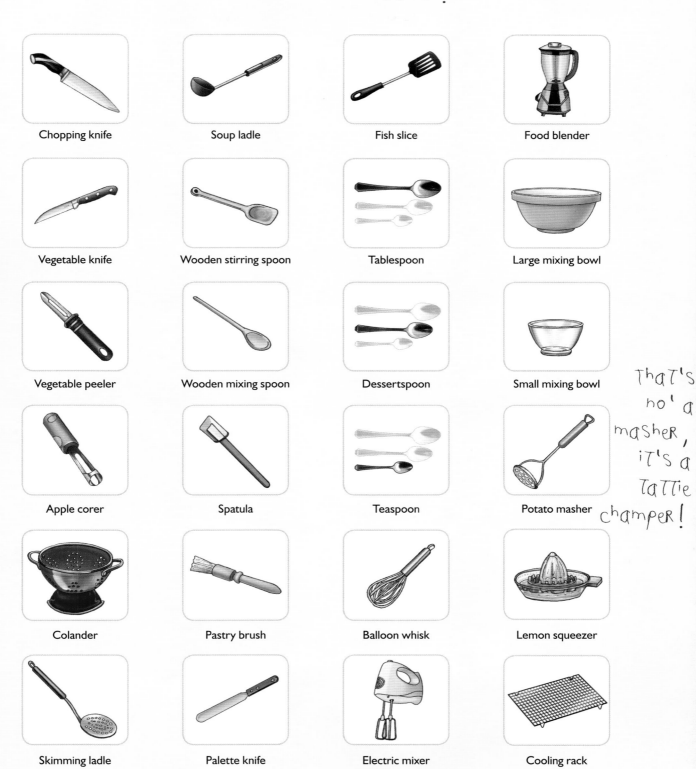

Chopping knife

Soup ladle

Fish slice

Food blender

Vegetable knife

Wooden stirring spoon

Tablespoon

Large mixing bowl

Vegetable peeler

Wooden mixing spoon

Dessertspoon

Small mixing bowl

Apple corer

Spatula

Teaspoon

Potato masher

Colander

Pastry brush

Balloon whisk

Lemon squeezer

Skimming ladle

Palette knife

Electric mixer

Cooling rack

That's no' a masher, it's a tattie champer!

9

Useful Measurements

Oven Temperatures

The temperature of every oven varies a little whether it's gas, electric or fan-assisted. So if the time your oven takes is a lot different from the time given in the recipe, it's important to make a note of this.

With non-fan-assisted ovens the hottest part is at the top and the coolest at the bottom. Keep baking tins in the middle of the shelf, away from the side to prevent burning. If the heat is coming from the back it's a good idea to turn baking trays halfway through the cooking.

Because fan-assisted ovens circulate the heat more evenly, making the whole oven hotter, this can reduce the baking time by 10 minutes in every hour. In the recipes where the oven temperature is important – as with delicate baking like a sponge cake – the time given in the recipes has a 10-minute variation to allow for this.

Gas Mark	Fahrenheit	Celsius	Description
¼	225	110	Very cool
½	250	130	Cool
1	275	140	Very low
2	300	150	Very low
3	325	170	Warm
4	350	180	Moderate
5	375	190	Moderately hot
6	400	200	Hot
7	425	220	Hot
8	450	230	Very hot
9	475	250	Very hot

Scales

Spring-operated scales are good for all kinds of measuring except baking where a few grams, more or less, could make a crucial difference.

The best scales for baking are digital scales because they are so precise. The digital display can usually convert from metric to imperial. You can also put the mixing bowl on the scale and add ingredients directly into the bowl. You can reset to zero, once you have weighed an item, then weigh other ingredients on top. This is a great time-saver.

Daphne keeps TRYing Tae Lose weighT
– buT iT keeps findin' her

yooceful meshuRements —

no. of biscuits I can fit in my mooth in one go — 5

no. of chips I can steal aff Iten's plate afore he notices — 4

Distance fae my room tae the fridge — 3 metres

Other Measures

1 teaspoon = 5 ml
1 tablespoon = 15 ml

Measuring based on the American cup
¼ cup = 2 fl oz or 60 ml
⅓ cup = 2½ fl oz or 80 ml
½ cup = 4 fl oz or 125 ml
1 cup = 8 fl oz or 250 ml

Conversion – metric/imperial
Always use either metric or imperial – do not mix the two.

Weight
15 g (½ oz)
25 g (1 oz)
40 g (1½ oz)
50 g (2 oz approx or 1¾ oz exact)
75 g (3 oz approx or 2¾ oz exact)
100 g (4 oz approx or 3½ oz exact)
125 g (4 oz approx or 4½ oz exact)
150 g (5 oz approx or 5½ oz exact)
175 g (6 oz)
200 g (7 oz)
225 g (8 oz)
250 g (8 oz approx or 9 oz exact)
275 g (9 oz approx or 9½ oz exact)
300 g (10 oz approx or 10½ oz exact)
325 g (11 oz approx or 11½ oz exact)
350 g (12 oz)
375 g (13 oz)
400 g (14 oz)
425 g (15 oz)
450 g (16 oz)
500 g (16 oz approx or 1 lb 2 oz exact)
600 g (1 lb 5 oz)
750 g (1 lb 10 oz
1 kg (2 lb approx or 2 lb 4 oz exact)
2.25 kg (5 lb)

Volume
15 ml (½ fl oz)
25 ml (1 fl oz)
50 ml (2 fl oz)
75 ml (3 fl oz approx or 2½ fl oz exact)
100 ml (3 fl oz approx or 3½ fl oz exact)
125 ml (4 fl oz)
150 ml (5 fl oz or ¼ pt)
175 ml (6 fl oz)
200 ml (7 fl oz)
250 ml (8 fl oz approx or 9 fl oz exact)
300 ml (10 fl oz or ½ pt)
325 ml (11 fl oz)
350 ml (12 fl oz)
400 ml (14 fl oz)
425 ml (15 fl oz or ¾ pt)
450 ml (16 fl oz)
475 ml (17 fl oz)
500 ml (20 fl oz approx or 18 fl oz exact)
600 ml (20 fl oz or 1 pt)
1 litre (2 pt approx or 1¾ pt exact)
1.2 litres (2 pt)
2 litres (3½ pt)
3 litres (5¼ pt)

What did the metric alien say?
Take me to your litre!

Horace's Guide to Food Types

There are three main groups of substances contained in food. These are needed by the body in differing amounts. They are carbohydrates, proteins and fats. In addition, the body requires fibre and vitamins and minerals. By eating a variety of different foods your body will get what it needs. Food is not only needed for daily life but has an important protective role in fighting and preventing disease, and prolonging life.

How do you keep flies oot o' The Kitchen?

Move The Rotten Fruit Tae The Sittin' Room.

CARBOHYDRATES

CARBOHYDRATES
– simple or complex
– provide energy for the body. The simplest forms are sugars, of which the most basic is glucose. All carbohydrates are broken down into glucose, which is absorbed and used by the body.

STARCHES are more complex carbohydrates. They take longer to be broken down, so provide a more gradual supply of glucose which is better for general good health.

SIMPLE SUGARS are found in cakes, processed foods and sweets etc. Starches are found in grains, bread, pasta, potatoes and other vegetables and fruits.

PROTEINS

SOURCES OF PROTEINS include beans, peas, pulses, whole grains, nuts, seeds, red meat, liver, kidney, poultry, fish, milk, cheese and dairy produce. Red meat is also a good source of essential amino acids.

PROTEINS are essential for repair and replacement of damaged cells and tissues. However, it is particularly important for growing children to receive plenty of protein in their diet since they are laying down the foundations of bones and muscles which must last for a lifetime.

The Three main Food Groups:

1) Sweeties
2) Crisps
3) Others

FATS

FATS play a vital role in the body. They provide important energy. Human beings store fat on their bodies.

SATURATED FATS, e.g. cholesterol, are found in meat and dairy products.

UNSATURATED FATS or oils are of two types: polyunsaturated and monounsaturated. Monounsaturated fats are found in olive oil, rapeseed oil, groundnut oil and some fish oils. Polyunsaturated fats are found in oily fish (e.g. mackerel, salmon, herring, trout), vegetable oils (e.g. corn, sunflower, safflower, rapeseed) and nuts and seeds. It is recommended that oily fish is eaten two or three times each week.

FIBRE

The most readily available sources of dietary FIBRE are foods containing wholewheat bran, such as wholemeal flour and bread, porridge oats, brown varieties of rice, pasta and spaghetti.

The general recommendation is that healthy adults should try to eat about 30 g of fibre each day. This is easily achieved by eating fibre-containing breakfast cereals, wholemeal bread, brown rice and pasta, fruits, vegetables and salads (at least five portions from the last three every day) and pulses (lentils, beans, peas, etc.).

VITAMINS AND MINERALS

VITAMINS are a group of organic substances that are required in minute quantities in the diet to maintain good health. They are involved in a large number of processes, including growth and repair of tissues and organs, metabolism of food and functioning of the immune, nervous, circulatory and hormonal systems.

MINERALS play a vital part in many metabolic processes. Some minerals, notably calcium and phosphorus, are present in significant amounts in the human body, mainly in bones and teeth. Others (e.g. iron, iodine and sodium) occur in extremely small quantities but are, nonetheless, very important.

WATER

The human body is largely composed of WATER (66 per cent) which is essential to all life processes. Health experts recommend that eight glasses of, preferably, plain water should be drunk each day as a minimum amount. This factor is frequently overlooked by people who are dieting and it is thought that mild dehydration, which is not good for the body, is a fairly common occurrence. It is interesting to note that the first 'weight' which is lost by someone embarking on a reduced-calorie diet is water!

HORACE got some vinegar in his ear — now he suffers from pickled hearing

Contents

Star Rating for Recipes

***** these are recipes which are very simple and don't need a lot of help

**** these are easy with only a few skills needed and a little help

*** these are still easy, but will need a few more skills and a bit more help

** these will need quite a bit of help from an adult if it's your first time making

* these will need quite a lot of help from an adult

Basic Skills

It's stating the obvious tae tell ye that basic skills are essential for ony aspiring cook — young or auld! Auntie Catherine will tell ye that if ye teach a bairn how tae chop an onion properly, how tae rub butter intae flour, separate an egg and so on, then those skills will stay with them for life. A bit like learnin' yer times tables in primary school.

Ye'll also find on pages 10 and 11 notes on measuring ingredients and on page 6 some kitchen rules, including a wee reminder aboot washin' up the dishes! Naebody's so keen on that! Hen still needs a daily dig in the ribs tae mind him tae wash the dishes. Left tae his own devices, he'd dirty every dish in the hoose afore he'd think o' getting oot the Fairy Liquid.

Granpaw seems tae think the solution tae washin' up is tae drop and break a' the dishes. Hmmm ... Men!

Happy cookin'!
fae Maw and Auntie Catherine

another basic skil
that maw kens
- the dreaded washin' up

16

How to peel and slice a potato finely

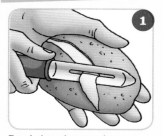
1
Peel the skin with a vegetable peeler.

2
Cut the potato in half.

3
Place on a chopping board cut side down.

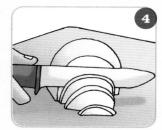
4
Cut very thin slices. Repeat for the second potato half.

Note: you do not need to dice a potato since it will break up as it cooks.

How to peel and cut a carrot into dice

1
Peel the skin with a vegetable peeler.

2
Cut off the top and tail with a chopping knife.

3
Cut the carrot in half, lengthways.

4
Cut again lengthways to make four sticks. Place the sticks together and chop into dice.

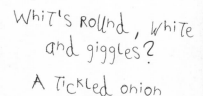

What's round, white and giggles?

A tickled onion

How to peel and chop an onion finely

1
Cut off the top end of the onion and leave the root on.

2
Slice the onion in half and remove the skin.

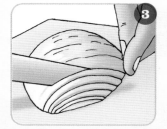
3
Place it flat side down on a chopping board and, holding the root end, slice in thin strips.

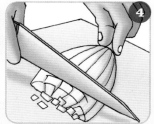
4
Still holding the root end, cut across in thin strips to make dice.

Note: if your eyes start watering do not rub them. Move away from the onion and wash your hands. Then rinse and dry your eyes.

17

How to chop a leek finely

1. Trim off the root and any damaged or tough leaves.

2. Hold up the leek from the root end and about 2 cm from the end push the end of a sharp vegetable knife all the way through the leek – sharp edge pointing away from the root end.

Why did The leek cross The Road?

IT saw a FORk Up ahead

3. Pull the knife downwards through the whole length of the leek.

4. Repeat the process, this time at right angles to the first cut so the whole stalk is cut into quarters.

5. Put under a running tap and wash thoroughly to remove any earth.

6. Place the whole sliced leek on a chopping board and, using a large chopping knife, chop the whole length of the leek finely (any size up to about 1 cm for broths).

How to peel and cut a quarter turnip into dice

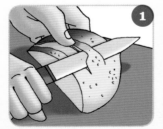

1. Place the flat side down on the board and slice off the thick outer layer of skin with a sharp knife.

2. Cut lengthways into slices with a chopping knife.

3. Cut slices into sticks.

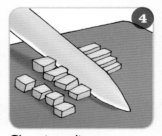

4. Chop into dice.

How to cut and rub butter into flour

1 Take the butter out of the fridge about an hour before it's required. It should not be too cold, when it's difficult to rub, or too soft, when it will melt and spoil the texture of the pastry or scones.

When makin' pastry make sure yer hands are nice an' cool
— Maw

2 Sift the flour into a bowl and cut the butter into small pieces, dropping it on top of the flour.

3 Pick up some of the mixture in your fingers and, holding your fingers together and with your hands upwards, start rubbing the flour and butter between your thumb and the tips of your fingers, letting it drop back into the bowl so the butter gets broken up into smaller and smaller pieces.

4 Continue till the mixture resembles fine breadcrumbs. Don't let the mixture get into the palms of your hands which are warm and will melt the butter. Keep rubbing till all the butter is in very small pieces and the mixture looks like fine breadcrumbs.

How to separate the yolk from the white of an egg

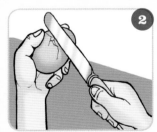

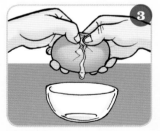

1 Get two small bowls, one for the yolk and one for the white, and a small table knife with a blunt edge. Hold the egg over the bowl to collect the white.

2 Hold the top and the bottom of the egg firmly between your thumb and forefingers of your left hand (if you are right-handed). Tap the middle of the egg firmly with the blunt edge of the knife to just crack the shell.

3 Hold the egg in two hands with thumb against thumb over the crack and gently pull the two halves apart. You might need to give the shell another tap if it does not break easily.

4 As the two halves separate, quickly catch the yolk in one half-shell. Tip the yolk from half-shell to half-shell allowing the white to run into the bowl underneath. If you drop any yolk into the white, don't worry, you can fish it out with a spoon but try not to break the yolk. Finally, tip the yolk into the other bowl.

19

How to make butter icing

You will need:

* 175 g unsalted butter at room temperature
* 250 g icing sugar or caster sugar
* Flavourings and food colourings

Before you start:

* Get a mixing bowl electric beater or wooden spoon sieve.

1 Put the butter into the bowl and beat to soften.

2 Sift half the icing sugar on top of the butter. Beat till well mixed.

3 Sift the remainder of the icing sugar into the mixture and beat till light and fluffy.

4 Add flavourings and food colourings of your choice.

How to make custard — runny or thick

You will need:

* 25 g custard powder for a runny custard
  or
* 50 g custard powder for a thick custard
* 1 heaped tablespoon caster or granulated sugar
* 600 ml whole milk

Before you start:

* Get a large mixing bowl wooden spoon medium saucepan balloon whisk or sieve.

1 Put the custard powder into the large mixing bowl with the sugar. Add about half a cup of milk and mix with the wooden spoon until you have a smooth paste with no lumps.

2 Put the rest of the milk in the saucepan and place over a medium heat. Warm until it is hot but not boiling.

3 Add the hot milk gradually, about a cupful at a time, to the custard mix in the bowl, stirring each time with the wooden spoon till smooth. When you have added all the milk, pour the custard back into the saucepan and put it onto a medium heat.

4 Simmer the custard gently till it thickens, stirring with the wooden spoon all the time. If there are any lumps in your custard, you can remove them by beating it with a balloon whisk or by putting it through a sieve.

How to make a green salad with wild greens

not nettles!

You will need:

Salad:
* 100 g small salad and herb leaves
* 50 g wild leaves or edible green weeds (see page 49)
* Small bunch of chives
* Quarter of a cucumber

Dressing:
* 1 tablespoon lemon juice
* 4 tablespoons olive oil
* Salt and pepper

Before you start:

* Get a large sieve or colander

  chopping board

  chopping knife

  large wooden or glass salad bowl

  small bottle with top, or jar with lid, for mixing dressing.

Put the leaves into the sieve and run under the cold tap, washing thoroughly. Drain.

Tear the leaves into bite-sized pieces. Chop the chives finely. Slice the cucumber thinly. Put everything into the salad bowl.

Pour lemon juice and olive oil into the bottle or jar and add salt and pepper. Shake to mix.

Serve the salad with the dressing. Shake the dressing again just before adding to the greens.

How to make sweet shortcrust pastry

You will need:

* 100 g unsalted butter at room temperature
* 50 g caster sugar
* 1 medium egg yolk (see page 19)
* 175 g plain flour

Before you start:

* Get a large mixing bowl

  wooden spoon or an electric mixer

  sieve

  clingfilm.

Beat the butter and sugar together in the large mixing bowl with a wooden spoon (or an electric mixer on a slow speed) till light and fluffy.

Add the egg yolk and beat for another minute to mix in.

Sift about half the flour into the mixture and beat till mixed in. Sift in the remainder of the flour and beat till it comes together into a firm paste. Do not overmix.

Knead to form into a smooth ball and wrap in cling film. Rest in the fridge for an hour before using.

A Piece and Jam

– and other snacks

Pieces are rerr and easy for bairns to mah' on their ain. If they mah' a bit o' a mess it's easily cleaned up! As well as slices of bread — plain or pan — try rolls, wraps, rice cakes and crispbread tae gie them a bit of variety.

We haTe Rice cakes
— TheY'Re made ooT o' POLYSTieReen

Fillings don't have to be boring. A quid haggisburger is a favourite at No. 10 and no just wi' the bairns. Oor Horace is no' keen on meat so his favourites are an open sandwich with some salad on top or a tasty tidbit o' cheese an' tomatoes on toast. Auntie Catherine gied us a recipe for cinnamon toast and this is oor Bairn's favourite noo — she aye thinks Christmas has come early when she gets it for her breakfast.

— Maw

The Jeely Piece Song

I'm a skyscraper wean; I live on the nineteenth flair,
But I'm no' gaun oot tae play ony mair,
Cause since we moved to Castlemilk, I'm wastin' away
Cause I'm gettin' wan meal less every day.

Oh ye cannae fling pieces oot a twenty-storey flat,
Seven hundred hungry weans will testify tae that.
If it's butter, cheese or jeely, if the breid is plain or pan,
The odds against it reaching earth are ninety-nine tae wan.

On the first day ma maw flung oot a daud o' Hovis broon;
It came skytin' oot the windae and went up insteid o' doon.
Noo every twenty-seven hours it comes back intae sight
Cause ma piece went intae orbit and became a satellite.

On the second day ma maw flung me a piece oot wance again.
It went and hut the pilot in a fast low-flying plane.
He scraped it aff his goggles, shouting through the intercom,
'The Clydeside Reds huv goat me wi' a breid-an-jeely bomb.'

On the third day ma maw thought she would try another throw.
The Salvation Army band was staunin' doon below.
'Onward Christian Soldiers' was the piece they should've played
But the oompahman was playing a piece an' marmalade.

We've wrote away to Oxfam to try an' get some aid,
An' a' the weans in Castlemilk have formed a 'piece-brigade'.
We're gonnae march to George's Square demanding civil rights
Like nae mair hooses ower piece-flinging height.

Adam McNaughtan, 1967

Why don't you starve in a desert?

Because of all the sand which is there

Horace's Food Fact File

'PAN' OR 'PLAIN' LOAF

In the early days of factory breadmaking in Scotland, most bread was made without bread tins. The balls of dough were simply placed beside one another on huge baking trays, so that when they came out the oven the bakers had to tear them apart. They had a thick 'sole' and a well-done crust on top while the sides were soft and doughy. These were called 'plain' or 'square' loaves.

But then the bakeries started using baking tins, which the bakers called 'pans', and the new loaf became a 'pan' loaf. It was considered to be a posh loaf, compared to the more rustic plain or square loaf. And anyone who tried to put on a posh accent was told they were speaking 'pan loaf'! But it's still great bread for a jeely piece. Just as a crispy Scotch morning roll with a holey middle is great for a bacon or haggis roll because soft rolls with doughy middles just don't work.

Jeely Piece

*****

feeds 1

You will need:

* 1 slice of a large pan loaf (see page 25)
* Butter for spreading
* Your favourite jam/jelly/thick honey/chocolate spread

Before you start:

* Get a plate table knife.

How to...

Spread the bread with butter.

Spread with your favourite jam/jelly/honey/chocolate spread.

Fold the bread over. Eat immediately.

folding The bRead keeps The flaVouR fae RUnnin' ooT!

WheRe do You go To PReseRve STRawbeRRies?

Jamaica!

Glebe Street Tips

A slice of a large pan loaf is essential because it's bendy. Check if your slice is bendy enough before spreading.

To make a cheesy piece: spread a slice of bread with butter. Grate 25–50 g of cheddar cheese onto one half of the slice and spread the other with pickle or chutney. Bend over as for a jeely piece.

Cinnamon Toast

***** feeds 1

You will need:

* 2 tablespoon brown sugar
* 1 teaspoon ground cinnamon
* 1 large slice of bread
* Butter for spreading

Before you start:

* Get a small bowl
  toaster
  table knife.
* Preheat the grill to fairly hot.

How to...

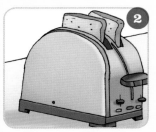

1. Mix the sugar and the cinnamon in the bowl.

2. Toast the bread in the toaster or under the grill. Remove.

3. Spread with butter.

4. Sprinkle some cinnamon sugar evenly on top.

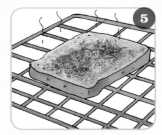

5. Put under the grill for about a minute to melt the butter.

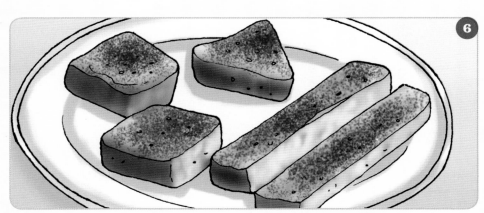

6. Remove and cut into squares, triangles or fingers. Eat while hot.

Glebe Street Tips

Experiment with mixed spice, ginger or nutmeg, starting with a small quantity till you find your favourite flavour.

Cinnamon is also very nice on Eggy Bread.

Cheese and Tomato on Toast

****

feeds 1

You will need:

* 50 g cheddar cheese
* 1 tomato
* 1 large slice of bread
* Salt and pepper

Before you start:

* Get a toaster
  grater
  plate
  chopping board
  sharp knife
  serving plate.
* Preheat the grill to fairly hot.

How to...

1 Put the bread into the toaster to toast both sides.

2 Grate the cheese onto a plate.

3 Cut the tomato into slices.

4 Put the toast onto the serving plate and, using half the grated cheese, cover the toast evenly with a layer of cheese.

5 Grill till the cheese has lightly melted.

6 Place 2–4 tomato slices on top of the cheese. Season with salt and pepper then cover the tomatoes with more grated cheese.

7 Grill till the cheese has lightly melted. Cut into fingers or triangles. Eat immediately.

Glebe Street Tips

Spread the toast with your favourite chutney, pickle, mustard or tomato purée before covering with cheese.

Use 2 tablespoons of your own tomato sauce (see page 52) instead of sliced tomato.

Bacon Roll

**** feeds **1**

You will need:

* 2 rashers Ayrshire middle bacon
* 1 fresh crusty roll

Before you start:

* Get a bread knife
  some kitchen foil
  kitchen tongs
  bread knife.
* Preheat the grill to
  fairly hot.

*How far does
the bacon roll?*

How to...

Cut open the roll with the bread knife.

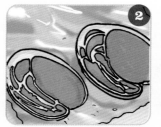

Place the bacon rashers side by side curled up in their round shape on the kitchen foil.

Place the foil on top of the grill pan grid.

Place under a hot grill for 2–3 minutes. Turn with the tongs and grill on the other side till crisp.

Using tongs, put the hot bacon onto the roll. Close, and press the two halves together. Eat immediately.

*Wit maks the tower o'
Pisa lean?
It never eats!*

Glebe Street Tips

Auntie Catherine says Ayrshire middle bacon is the ideal shape for a bacon roll but other kinds of bacon can be folded to fit.

Avoid rolls with very doughy insides. The perfect roll is a crispy Scotch roll, with a light 'holey' interior and crunchy crust.

Haggisburger

***** **feeds 1**

You will need:

* 1 slice of butcher's haggis
* 1 large soft roll
* Chutney or pickles
* Lettuce or other salad leaves
* Olive oil

Before you start:

* Get a small piece of kitchen foil
  kitchen tongs
  bread knife
  table knife.
* Preheat the grill to fairly hot.

How to...

1 Place the haggis on a sheet of kitchen foil and put on the grill pan grid.

2 Put under a hot grill and cook for 2–3 minutes on one side. Remove and turn with the tongs. Grill for another 2–3 minutes.

3 The timing will depend on the thickness of the slice. To check if it's cooked through, make a cut with a knife and open slightly.

4 Cut open the roll with the bread knife.

5 Spread one half of the roll with chutney or pickles.

6 Put the haggis on top and cover with salad leaves. Sprinkle with a few drops of olive oil.

7 Close the roll, press the two halves together and eat immediately.

Glebe Street Tips

The slice of haggis can also be fried. In which case, you can finely chop an onion (see page 17) and fry in a tablespoon of oil till crisp and golden brown. Then fry the haggis. Pile the onion on top of the haggis in the roll.

Boiled Egg & Toast Soldiers

***** feeds 1

You will need:

* 1 or 2 medium eggs
* Cold water
* 1 teaspoon of salt
* 1 large slice of bread or 2 small slices
* Butter for spreading
* Salt and pepper

Before you start:

* Get a small saucepan timer
  table knife
  tablespoon
  egg cup.

How to...

Which Regiment are These so-called sojers fae?

1 Put the egg (or eggs) into the pan and cover with cold water by about 2 cm. Add a teaspoon of salt to prevent the shell cracking.

2 Put on a high heat and bring to the boil. Reduce heat to a simmer and set the timer:
very runny – 2 minutes;
yolk still runny in the middle – 3 minutes;
hard boiled – 4 minutes.

3 While the egg is boiling, toast the bread in the toaster or under the grill. Remove. Spread with butter.

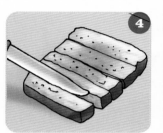

4 Cut the toast into 'soldiers'.

Why did The Fermer feed his chickens haggis?

So They'd Lay Scotch eggs

5 Use the tablespoon to lift out the egg and place it in an egg cup.

6 Cut the top off the egg. Season with salt and pepper. Dip the toast soldiers into the runny yolk.

Glebe Street Tips

Eggs should be at room temperature before they are boiled.

Putting the eggs into cold water and bringing them slowly to the boil helps to prevent the shell cracking.

If you want to eat a hard-boiled egg cold, for example in a salad or a sandwich, cool the egg in cold water immediately after cooking and the shell will come off much more easily.

If your eggs float when you put them into the pan of cold water, they are not fresh.

A Plate of Broth

– a meal-in-a-plate

RECIPES IN THIS SECTION:

**** Green Pea Soup with Mint
*** Lentil and Bacon Broth
*** Scotch Broth
*** Tattie and Leek Broth with Kale or Nettles
*** Mussel Broth

Makin' soup teaches a bairn that they can always mak' something tae keep them goin' for a couple of days – although a pot of soup only tends tae last a day mind when Daphne's aboot! Tattie soup made wi' guid floury spuds is Granpaw's No. 1 and he's also partial tae ham and lentil soup made wi' a guid ham hough.

Tasty green pea soup made wi' fresh peas is just right for summer. The Bairn loves tae help me pop the peapods. She'll eat dozens right oot the pod if I let her. I hae my ain special favourite – tattie and leek broth wi' nettles. Aye, real nettles I'm talkin' aboot – picked right outside the But an' Ben. Auntie Catherine is a real keen forager when she visits oor holiday hoose. Then there's Paw's favourite filler, Scotch broth, and last but by nae means least, try the braw seafood soup, made wi' ony manner of fishy bits an' pieces, like mussels or cockles.

— Maw

Horace's Food Fact File

SCOTCH BROTH

In the days when a deep plate of broth was your dinner, a huge cast-iron cauldron was hooked onto a chain and hung over the fire in every Scottish home. And into it went whatever fresh vegetables, greens and herbs were available, so you could tell what time of year it was by what was in the pot. Barley and oatmeal were the nation's main broth-thickening grains. Meat or fish, for extra flavour, were sometimes plentiful and sometimes very scarce but your deep plate always had a bit of everything in it.

For cooks, though, the great thing about the big pot was that there was enough broth to last several days. It saved on both time and fuel. And when there was plenty food, there might also be a large piece of meat or a chicken, cooked in the broth, which could be used for more meals.

All over the country, cooks developed a good sense of how to make a very tasty pot of broth. So much so, that when people came to visit they were very impressed with our Scotch broths and the Scots became known around the world as masters of the broth pot.

WAITER – THERE'S A FLY IN MY SOUP!

nO THERE'S nO' – ThaT'S an essenshull ViTamin bee!

GRANPAW is a bROTh o' a bOY (he has been FOR nEARLY a cenTURY!)

Green Pea Soup with Mint

**** **feeds 4**

You will need:

* 500 g peas, fresh shelled or frozen
* 600 ml water
* 100 g streaky bacon rashers
* Bunch of fresh mint leaves
* 100 ml single cream
* Salt and pepper

Before you start:

* Get a large pot with a lid
  sheet of kitchen foil
  liquidiser or food processor
  soup ladle
  chopping board
  chopping knife
  spoon and cup.
* Warm 4 soup plates before serving.
* Preheat the grill to medium hot.

How to...

1. Put the peas into the pot and add the water.
Put over a medium heat and bring to the boil. Simmer for about 2 minutes. Remove from the heat and leave to cool a little.

2. Place the bacon rashers on a sheet of foil, put on the grill rack and grill the bacon for 2–3 minutes on either side. Remove the grill pan and leave the bacon to cool.

3. When the peas and water are cool enough, ladle into the liquidiser.

4. Keeping back 4 sprigs of mint, tear off the remaining mint leaves from the stalks and add to the peas in the liquidiser. Whizz to blend.

5. Put the bacon onto the chopping board and chop roughly.

6. Add the chopped bacon to the blended soup and whizz up to make a smooth purée. Return to the pan.

7. Add the cream and mix through. Reheat on a medium heat. To adjust the seasoning: take out a spoonful of soup and cool in a cup before tasting. Season to taste with salt and pepper.

8. Ladle the soup into the soup plates and finish off with a sprig of mint. Serve.

Glebe Street Tips

Leave out the bacon and instead of water use the cooking liquid from boiling a piece of ham for more flavour. Taste the liquid before using – it may have to be diluted if it's too salty.

In summer: just before serving add some ice cubes for a chilled version.

Call'd soup? I would send that back.

Lentil and Bacon Broth

*** feeds **6-8** to do **2 days**

You will need:

* 2 large carrots
* ¼ medium turnip
* 2 large floury potatoes
* 2 medium onions
* 3 rashers streaky bacon
* 2 tablespoons sunflower oil
* 175g red lentils
* 1 tin chopped tomatoes
* 2 litres water
* 2 tablespoons parsley
* Salt and pepper

Before you start:

* Get a vegetable peeler
  chopping board
  small vegetable knife
  chopping knife
  large saucepan with a lid
  wooden stirring spoon
  spoon and cup
  soup ladle.
* Warm 4 soup plates before serving.

How to...

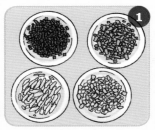

1 Prepare the vegetables: peel and finely dice the carrots and the turnip; peel and thinly slice the potatoes; and finely chop the onions (see pages 17 and 18).

2 Chop the bacon finely.

3 Put the oil into the pan over a medium heat till hot but not smoking. To test if the oil is hot enough: drop a piece of the bacon into the pan. If the oil is ready, the bacon should start sizzling.

4 Add the bacon and cook gently till crisp but not browned.

5 Add all the fresh vegetables. Stir well for a few minutes over a low heat.

6 Put the lid on and leave on a very low heat for 5 minutes. Stir again. Leave for another 5 minutes. During this time the vegetables will soften and absorb the flavour from the bacon fat.

7 Add the lentils and chopped tomatoes. Stir well.

8 Add the water and turn up the heat. Bring to the boil. Reduce the heat and simmer very gently with the lid on till all the vegetables are cooked. Stir occasionally.

Check after simmering for 45 minutes to see if vegetables are soft.

Meanwhile, finely chop the parsley.

To adjust the seasoning: take out a spoonful of the soup and cool in a cup before tasting. Season to taste with salt and pepper.

Put chopped parsley into heated soup plates then ladle broth on top. Serve with oatcakes or bannocks.

When The doctor asks Tae Tak' yer pulse, is he really after yer lentil soup?

Knock! Knock!

Who's There?

Lentil!

Lentil who?

Lentil my change to my friend got none left for the bus hame!

Glebe Street Tips

Instead of bacon and water, you can use the liquid from boiling a knuckle of ham or a joint of ham. Chop some of the cooked ham to put into the soup at the end of the recipe (after step 9) and heat through thoroughly. You will also have some meat for another meal the next day.

If you want more flavour: add a dessertspoon of black treacle and the juice of half a lemon when adding the chopped tomatoes (step 7).

Scotch Broth

*** feeds **6-8** / to do **2 days**

You will need:

* 50 g pearl barley
* 25 g split peas
* 25 g red lentils
* 2 litres cold water
* 350 g neck, shoulder or shank of mutton or lamb, or beef hough or nineholes
* 2 carrots
* ¼ medium turnip
* 2 large floury potatoes (see page 44)
* 2 leeks or 2 stalks of celery
* 1 teaspoon sugar
* Salt and pepper to taste
* 2 tablespoons chopped parsley

Before you start:

* Get a sieve
  large pot with a lid
  skimming ladle
  kitchen tongs
  plate
  vegetable peeler
  small vegetable knife
  chopping board
  chopping knife
  spoon and cup
  soup ladle.
* Warm 4 soup plates before serving.

How to...

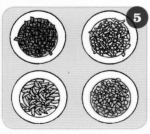

1 Rinse the barley, peas and lentils in a sieve under the tap. Put them into the pot with the cold water and leave overnight or for a few hours.

2 Add the meat, bring to the boil and take off any foam with a skimming ladle. Reduce the heat to a gentle simmer.

3 Put on the lid and continue to simmer the soup for about 1½ hours or until the meat is falling off the bones.

4 Remove the meat and bones from the broth using the tongs and leave on a plate until cool enough to handle.

5 While the broth is cooking, prepare the vegetables: peel and finely dice the carrots and turnip (see pages 17 and 18); peel and thinly slice the potatoes (see page 17); finely chop the leeks (see page 18) or the celery.

6 Add all the vegetables – except the green top of the leek – and the sugar to the broth. Continue to simmer over a low heat until the vegetables are tender.

7 Remove all of the edible meat from the cooled meat and bones, chop it up finely and return to the broth.

8 Add the finely chopped green leek and simmer for a minute or two until it softens. To adjust the seasoning: take out a spoonful of the broth and cool in a cup before tasting. Season to taste with salt and pepper.

Put some chopped parsley in each of the heated soup plates. Ladle the broth into the soup plates and serve with oatcakes or bannocks.

AUnTie CaTHeRiHe — WHiT's THis?

IT's bean soUp.

AYe — bUT WHAT is iT noW?

WHiT did Ye geT Up To TH'daY, HoRace?

Weel — I washed the kitchen floor, scrubbed the front step, cleaned the dishes and wiped them dry! Then I polished aff the biscuits in the cupboard!

Glebe Street Tips

Greens (leek tops, kale or nettles) should not be cooked too long or they lose some of their vitamin C content as well as their bright green colour.

Instead of cooking the potatoes in the broth, boil some floury potatoes separately and put one or two – still in their skins if you like – in the centre of each soup plate to make an island.

Grate the carrot and turnip instead of dicing – they will cook more quickly.

Use 100 g of packet broth mix instead of the barley and peas.

Add a bunch of fresh herbs. (See Glebe Street Tips on page 40.)

Tattie and Leek Broth with Kale or Nettles

*** **feeds 6-8** **to do 2 days**

You will need:

* Knuckle of ham or a piece of boiling ham
* 2 litres cold water
* 1 kg floury potatoes (see page 44)
* 600 g leeks
* 100 g tender young kale or young nettles
* Salt and pepper

Before you start:

* Get a large pot with a lid
  skimming ladle
  vegetable peeler
  small vegetable knife
  chopping board
  chopping knife
  wooden stirring spoon
  large plate
  spoon and cup
  soup ladle.
* Warm 4 soup plates before serving.

How to...

1 Put the ham and the cold water into the large pot. Bring to the boil and take off any surface foam with the skimming ladle. Simmer for about an hour with the lid on.

2 Meantime, wash, peel and slice the potatoes thinly (see page 17). Wash and chop the leeks finely (see page 18) and separate the green from the white leek.

3 Add the potatoes and chopped white leek to the pot. Stir with a wooden spoon and leave to simmer gently till the potatoes are cooked.

4 Remove the ham and leave on a plate till cool enough to handle. Remove any edible meat and chop finely. Add to the broth.

GRANPAW is an auld ham!

5 Prepare the kale or nettles: use only young leaves and remove from stalk. Wash and chop the leaves finely. If using nettles, wear rubber gloves to pick, wash and chop.

6 Add the chopped green leek and kale or nettles to the broth, and heat through for a few minutes. Remove the pot from the heat.

7 To adjust the seasoning: take out a spoonful of broth and cool in a cup before tasting. Season to taste with salt and pepper.

8 Ladle the broth into the warmed soup plates and serve with oatcakes or bannocks.

BUNCH OF FRESH HERBS: to add a special herb flavour and aroma, make up a bunch of fresh herbs using small bunches of thyme and parsley, also a bay leaf. You can also use a few leaves of wild garlic in springtime. Put them inside the outer leaves of a piece of leek or inside a stick of celery and bind them together with sewing thread. Add to the broth with the cold water. Remove before serving.

Glebe Street Tips

NETTLES AND KALE: in the days before you could buy salad greens from the greengrocer, lots of Scottish back gardens had a nettle-patch. Everyone got very excited when it sprang into life in March and they started picking the first green shoots. Of course they had to protect their hands while picking and chopping. Soon they had enough nettle greens for a pot of 'nettle kail' – a springtime tonic, making them feel better after the long winter months when greens were scarce. Another old Scottish vegetable was 'kail', now known as 'kale'. In its heyday, it was such an important ingredient in the nation's daily pot of broth that the vegetable patch was known as the 'kailyard' though they grew lots of other plants besides kale. For Scots in the past, kale's special quality was that it did not wilt and die in the frosty winter but continued to provide greens when they were very scarce.

Mussel Broth

*** **feeds 4**

You will need:

* 2 kg mussels in their shells
* 300 ml water
* 2 tablespoons chopped parsley

Before you start:

* Get a large pot with a lid
  wooden spoon
  colander or large sieve
  large bowl
  spoon and cup
  soup ladle.
* Warm 4 soup bowls
  before serving.

How to...

1. Scrub the mussels clean. Remove any 'beards' (the hairy bit that the mussel used to cling to the rock). Discard any mussels that are open and stay open when tapped since they are no longer alive.

2. Put the water into the pot over a high heat and bring to the boil. Add half the cleaned mussels. Cover with the lid.

3. Boil for about 60 seconds. Remove the lid and stir or shake the mussels. Put the lid back on and leave boiling for another 60 seconds.

4. Check again. Remove from the heat immediately they are all opened.

5. Drain the mussels into a colander or sieve, catching the liquid (called mussel bree) in the large bowl.

6. Remove a spoonful of the liquid and cool in a small cup. Taste for saltiness. Add more water if it tastes too salty. Return the liquid to the pot. Heat up until just simmering.

7. Put the cooked mussels into the bowl and cover with a lid to keep hot. Repeat with the remainder of the mussels.

8. When both lots of mussels are cooked, put them into the warmed soup bowls. Ladle over enough boiling liquid to half-fill the bowls.

Why can ye ho' lift yer fishin' net oot the watter?

Cos I've pulled a mussel!

Sprinkle with the chopped parsley.
Serve with crusty bread and spare bowls for the shells.

There is a species of mussel, native to Scotland, called the Clabbie Dubh (pronounced Clabby doo). They are large horse mussels and live on rocky shorelines.

What fish goes up the river at 100 miles an hour?

A motor pike!

Glebe Street Tips

* Mussels spawn between May and August so are not at their best during these months.
* Use cockles instead of mussels.
* Add some cream for a richer broth.
* Instead of parsley use chopped spring onions. Or in springtime gather some wild garlic leaves and chop them just before serving.
* To add more flavour: begin by melting a knob of butter in the large pot and adding a very finely chopped small onion. Cook till just soft then add 3–4 finely chopped rashers of bacon and continue to cook till the bacon is cooked. Add 2 cloves of peeled and crushed garlic. Then continue by following the mussel broth recipe on these pages.

Dinners

– main courses

STEEPIES

TRY Daphne's new Recipe FOR dieT meaTloaf . . . iT's dieT because You won'T eaT much . . . blech!

Horace's Food Fact File
'FLOURY' OR 'WAXY' POTATOES

At one time Scottish farmers used to trundle their handcarts through the city streets selling dry, 'floury', boiled-in-their-skins potatoes.

'Mealie tatties,' they cried out, as they went from street to street. Those were the days when all Scottish tatties were 'mealie', or 'floury' as we call them today. They had a low water content and a high floury (dry) content and made the best mash and chips.

English 'waxy' potatoes, on the other hand, had more water and their flavour was not highly rated. But the waxy potatoes' worst sin was that they made a pot of lumpy mash, not to mention terrible chips!

Not so long ago, however, some potato farmers in Scotland began to abandon the old Scots 'mealie tatties' and they became very hard to find. They were more expensive to grow, since they did not produce so many potatoes per acre, and this meant they were also a bit more expensive to buy. Luckily, there were other tattie farmers who liked a good pot of mash and they carried on growing floury varieties, such as Kerr's Pink, Golden Wonder, Desiree, King Edward, British Queen (Irish), Edzell Blue, Arran Victory, Arran Consul, Epicure, Dunbar Rover or Dunbar Standard and Maris Piper, so we Scots can still make the best mash and chips ever!

What did the big tomato say to the wee tomato?
You go on and I'll ketchup.

As much as he cannae get enough o' the stuff, Paw Broon couldna mak' mince an' tatties tae save his life, so teachin' bairns tae mak' Scotland's favourite dish will set them up for life. It's an essential dish – just ask Oor Wullie! Stovies is anither essential dish. And, as ye'll see, ye can even mak' stovies wi' leftovers – no' that there's many leftovers in No. 10 Glebe Street, I hasten tae add. Horace is no sae fond o' meat, so there's a pasta and tomato sauce meal, and for the Twins, a pizza recipe. (See the bakin' section o' the book on how tae mak' the bread dough.) Auntie Catherine suggests how tae mak' your ain salad choosing your favourite ingredients. Even fussy bairns will be happy tae eat all their ain hard work! Herring or mackerel in oatmeal finishes aff this section. Granpaw tells me his grandfather was eatin' herring in oatmeal when Queen Victoria was a nipper.

— Maw

Chicken Stovies

✳✳✳✳

feeds **4**

You will need:

* 2 medium onions
* 1 kg floury potatoes (see p. 44)
* 4 fresh chicken thighs or 8 fresh drumsticks
* 1 tablespoon plain flour
* 1 tablespoon sunflower oil
* 25 g butter
* 2 level teaspoons salt
* 250 ml cup water or chicken stock

Before you start:

* Get either a casserole (1–1½ litre) with a tight-fitting lid which can be used on the stove and in the oven, or a frying pan and an earthenware casserole

  chopping knife

  chopping board

  2 plates

  wooden spoon

  pastry brush.
* Warm 4 plates before serving.
* Preheat the oven for 5–10 minutes to Gas 4/180°C.

How to...

Finely chop the onions (see page 17). Peel the potatoes and slice thinly (see page 17).

Put the flour on the plate and turn the chicken joints in the flour till they are well coated.

Put the casserole (or frying pan) onto a medium heat and heat the oil and butter in the pan. The oil should be hot but not smoking hot. To test: drop in a piece of onion and if it sizzles the oil is ready.

Add the chicken and brown gently until the skin is crisp and golden brown. This should take 5–10 minutes. Remove to a plate.

Put half the onions and potatoes, mixed together, in the casserole. Sprinkle lightly with salt. Sprinkle over any leftover flour.

Place the chicken on top. Sprinkle with a little more salt.

Cover with the remaining onions and potatoes. Sprinkle with the remainder of the salt.

Pour water or stock into the casserole. Put on the lid.

Why was the potato arrested on the motorway?

It broke the spud limit!

Put the casserole into
the oven and bake for
an hour, or cook on the
stove over a low heat for
about an hour.

Take off the lid and serve with a green vegetable or
sprinkle over some chopped parsley.

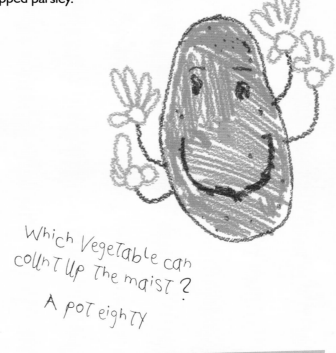

Which vegetable can
count up the maist?

A pot eighty

Glebe Street Tips

This is a slow, moist method for cooking the tougher meat of the thighs or drumsticks of birds such as chicken, duck, pheasant and other game birds.

It's traditionally used for leftover meat and gravy from a roast: put the meat in layers with the onions and potatoes and pour over the gravy (made up to 250 ml). Or use a special butcher's tub of dripping and gravy made up for stovies.

Make the above recipe in a slow cooker.

Instead of chicken, use lamb chops.

Frying the chicken in butter gives the best flavour, but meat dripping or vegetable oils can be used (with the exception of extra virgin olive oil which should be kept for salads).

Use chicken stock from boiling up the bones from a roast chicken.

Make-Your-Own Salad

**** feeds 4

Choose from:

Vegetable ingredients (vegetables, leaves and flowers):

* Any kind of lettuce
* Watercress or cress
* Rocket
* Nasturtium leaves and flowers
* Herbs: parsley, dill, chives, basil
* Cherry tomatoes
* Celery
* Cucumber
* Spring onion
* Avocado
* Green, red or yellow peppers
* Young carrot
* Cooked beetroot
* Leftover boiled potatoes, boiled rice, pasta
* Cooked beans, red, kidney or haricot
* Wild leaves (see Horace's Food Fact File, opposite)

Before you start:

* Get a colander chopping board vegetable knife chopping knife 4 large dinner plates enough dishes/ plates/boards to hold all your prepared ingredients.

Dressings:

* Extra virgin olive oil and vinegar or lemon juice
* Mayonnaise

Protein ingredients:

* 4 eggs
* 150 g cheese: cheddar, cottage, brie, blue cheese
* 150 g meat: cold ham, cooked chicken, leftover roast meat
  or
* 150 g fish: smoked mackerel, sweet-pickled herring, tinned tuna, sardines

How to...

1. Wash and dry all the leafy and vegetable ingredients using the colander.

2. Tear up large leaves into bite-sized pieces. Remove any tough stalks.

3. Chop celery, cucumber and spring onions finely.

4. Cut the avocado in half and remove the stone. Scoop out the flesh and cut into slices.

5. Cut the top and the bottom off the green, red or yellow peppers. Make a cut through the side and open up. Cut out the seed core. Slice into bite-sized pieces.

6. Peel and grate the carrot. Grate or slice the beetroot.

7. Chop the potatoes into bite-sized cubes.

8. Hard-boil the eggs (see page 31). Remove their shells and slice.

Have you seen the lettuce bat?

No, but I've seen the salad bowl!

Put the cheeses, cold meats or fish onto plates or wooden chopping boards.

Choose your favourite dressing.

Place everything in the middle of the table. Start creating your own salad.

Horace's Food Fact File

Wild greens or weeds: these are very strong plants that push out the weaker plants in cultivated gardens. They are usually pulled out and thrown away but you can make a very interesting salad from edible weeds. The list for the year includes: sorrel, dandelion, red and white clover, chickweed, fat hen, daisy, ground elder, silver weed, hogweed, rosebay willowherb, lesser celandine, yarrow, comfrey, wild garlic and goose grass. As a rule, it's better to use tender new leaves rather than tough old ones and you should use them before, or during, flowering but not after when the plant is past its best. Wild garlic's best flavour is in its young springtime leaves and flowers rather than its bulb. Always get an adult to help you identify plants and if in any doubt — don't eat.

Turn tae page 112 for ma list o' books tae help wi' foragin' for wild greens.

Glebe Street Tips

Avoid clashing flavours such as chicken and sardines.

Herbs are fairly pungent so do not use in large quantities.

Lettuces are quite bland so they work well as background ingredients with pungent herbs.

Starchy ingredients such as potatoes, pasta, beans and rice are good background ingredients; also hard-boiled eggs, especially with parsley, spring onions and chives.

Grated beetroot is best with an oil and vinegar dressing rather than mayonnaise and it mixes well with piquant pickled herring.

49

Mince and Tatties

***

feeds 4

OOR OTHER national dish

You will need:

For the mince:
* 2 onions
* 2 carrots
* 2 tablespoons sunflower oil
* 500 g steak mince
* 1 level teaspoon salt
* Water to cover

For champit (mashed) tatties:
* 1 kg floury potatoes, washed (if possible: Golden Wonder, Maris Piper or Kerr's Pink – see page 44)
* 1 level teaspoon salt
* Water to cover
* 25–50 g butter
* 100 ml milk
* Salt and pepper

Before you start:

* Get 2 medium-sized saucepans with lids
  chopping board
  vegetable knife
  chopping knife
  wooden spoon
  fork
  spoon and saucer
  colander
  potato masher.
* Warm 4 plates before serving.

How to...

To make the mince:

1 Peel and chop the onions finely (see page 17). Peel the carrots (see page 17) and slice them into rings.

2 Put a pan on a medium heat and add the oil. Heat the oil until it's hot but not smoking hot. To test if the oil is hot enough: drop in a piece of onion and when it sizzles the oil is ready.

3 Add onion and fry gently over a medium heat, stirring now and then until it begins to brown. This will take 10–15 minutes.

4 When the onion is lightly browned, push it to one side of the pan and add the mince. Break it up with a fork. Continue to brown the mince and onion together until there's no liquid in the pan and the mince is dry and browned.

5 Add carrots, salt and enough water to just cover. Bring to a simmer over a low heat. Cover and cook for about half an hour.

6 To adjust the seasoning: take out a spoonful of mince and cool on a saucer before tasting. Season to taste with salt and pepper.

Daphne Broon

Hen BRC

To make the tatties:

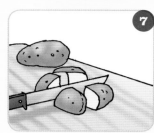

7 Wash the potatoes then cut up any large ones so that they are all roughly the same size and will take the same amount of time to cook.

8 Put them into the other saucepan and cover with water. Add salt and bring to the boil over a high heat. Cover with lid. Reduce the heat and simmer gently till they are just soft.

9 Floury tatties will soften quickly so check after 15 minutes: pierce one with a sharp knife which should go in easily when they are ready.

10 Remove the pan from the heat and carefully drain off the water through a sieve or colander, leaving the potatoes in the pan. Leave the lid off and let them dry out and cool a little.

11 To peel the potatoes: put the potato on a plate, hold in place with a fork and peel off the skin with a knife.

12 Return the peeled potatoes to the pan with the butter and milk and mash with the potato masher till smooth. Beat with a wooden spoon to make them creamy.

13 To adjust the seasoning: take out a spoonful of mashed potato and cool on a saucer before tasting. Season to taste with salt and pepper.

14 Serve with the mince.

Mince and Tatties

I dinna like hail tatties
Pit on my plate o mince
For when I tak my denner
I like them baith at yince.

Sae mash and mix the tatties
Wi mince into the mashin
And sic a tasty denner
Will aye be voted 'Smashin!'

JK Annand (1908–1983)

Glebe Street Tips

For very creamy tatties, add 2–3 tablespoons single or double cream to the mashed potatoes and beat with a balloon whisk, or an electric beater, till the potatoes are very light and creamy.

Instead of tatties, you can make doughboys (dumplings). Mix 125 g self-raising flour with 50 g prepared suet and 2 tablespoons of chopped parsley or chives. Add salt and pepper to taste and mix with enough water to make a soft elastic dough. Then drop spoonfuls of the dough on top of the mince. Cook with the lid on while the mince is cooking until the doughboys are light and cooked through (open one up to make sure).

For a mince and tomato sauce for pasta: cook the mince as above, missing out the carrots but adding a tablespoonful of tomato purée when browning the mince and onion. Also add a tin of chopped tomatoes to the mince before covering with water. Then cook for about half an hour as before. You can also add a tablespoonful of chopped fresh marjoram or oregano (if using dried just use a teaspoonful) at the same time as the chopped tomatoes.

Pasta with Tomato Sauce

*** feeds **4**

You will need:

Tomato sauce
* 2 onions
* 4 rashers streaky bacon
* 2 tablespoons sunflower oil
* 1–2 tablespoons tomato purée
* 2 tins chopped tomatoes
* 1 heaped teaspoon Demerara sugar
* 1 tablespoon fresh oregano or marjoram (or 1 teaspoon if using dried)
* Salt and pepper

Pasta
* Water
* 1 teaspoon salt
* 300 g of your favourite pasta
* 1 tablespoon virgin olive oil
* 100 g extra-mature cheddar cheese
* Black pepper, freshly ground
* A few fresh basil leaves

Before you start:

* Get a large frying pan for the sauce
  chopping board
  chopping knife
  wooden stirring spoon
  spoon and small dish
  3-litre pot with a lid for the pasta
  colander or large sieve
  black pepper grinder.
* Warm a large serving dish and 4 plates before serving.

How to...

To make the tomato sauce:

1 Peel and finely chop the onions (see page 17). Chop the bacon into small cubes.

2 Put the frying pan over a medium heat and add the oil. Heat till hot but not smoking hot. To test if the oil is ready: drop in a piece of bacon and when it sizzles the oil is ready.

3 Fry the bacon till crisp.

4 Add the onions and continue to fry. Keep turning, till they are softened and lightly browned.

5 Add the tomato purée and stir well. Cook for a minute.

6 Add the chopped tomatoes, sugar, oregano or marjoram and bring to a simmer. Simmer for 10–15 minutes without a lid to reduce the liquid and concentrate the flavour.

7 To adjust the seasoning: take out a spoonful of the sauce and cool a little before tasting. Season to taste with salt and pepper.

What's a teddy bear's favourite pasta? Tagliateddy!

To cook the pasta:

First grate the cheese and set aside. Fill the pot ½ –¾ full with water. Put on a high heat and bring up to the boil. Add the pasta and a teaspoon of salt. Stir with a wooden spoon to prevent the pasta sticking together.

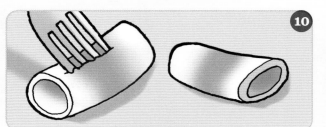

Reduce the heat and simmer without the lid. Check the pasta. It can take anything from between 8 to 15 minutes to cook.

To test: remove a piece of pasta after 8–10 minutes. Leave to cool and cut in half. The outer part will be creamy but there will still be a darker uncooked bit in the middle. Taste to check the texture. If the hard bit in the middle is too hard return to the pan and continue cooking. If it is not too hard but still has a slight 'bite' the pasta is ready. If it's very soft, you've cooked it too much. Don't worry it will still taste okay. Better luck next time.

Put the colander into the sink. Remove the pot from the heat and empty the pasta into the colander. Give it a good shake to get rid of all the water.

Return the pasta to the pot and add the tablespoon of olive oil to prevent it sticking together. Stir it to mix in the olive oil.

Put into the heated serving dish. Add the tomato sauce on top. Sprinkle with the grated cheese and some roughly torn fresh basil leaves. If you like black pepper, serve your pasta with a little freshly ground black pepper.

How dae ye fix a broken tomato? Use Tomato paste!

Glebe Street Tips

Use leftover fancy-shaped pasta for a cold pasta salad.

A quick-and-easy method for pasta and tomato sauce is to simply mix the hot pasta with chopped fresh tomatoes, season with salt and pepper and sprinkle with lots of cheese and some roughly torn basil leaves.

Grilled Herring in Oatmeal

*** **feeds 4**

You will need:

* 4 whole, gutted herring or mackerel or 4 fillets
* 3–4 tablespoons medium, coarse or pinhead oatmeal
* 1 teaspoon salt
* 2 tablespoons sunflower oil
* 2 lemons, halved
* Creamy mashed potatoes (see page 51)
* 2 tablespoons chopped chives

Before you start:

* Get a large plate small, sharp knife fish slice.
* Line a baking tray with kitchen foil.
* Preheat the grill to high.
* Warm 4 plates before serving.

Can we no' hae chips wi this fish, maw?

How to...

1 Put the oatmeal on the plate and add the salt. Mix well.

2 Wash the fish. If the fish is whole, make two or three slashes with a small, sharp knife through the thickest part on either side of the fish (this allows the heat to penetrate better).

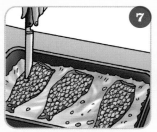

3 Press the fish firmly into the oatmeal so that the oatmeal sticks to the skin.

4 Put the fish on the baking tray. Fillets should be flesh side down. Drizzle over some oil.

5 Put the fish under the grill and cook on one side for 3–5 minutes depending on how thick the fish is. Fillets will cook faster than whole fish.

6 Remove the baking tray from under the grill and turn the fish over using the fish slice. Replace under the grill and cook the other side. Sprinkle with more oatmeal if necessary.

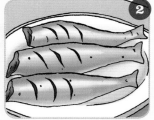

7 To test when the fish is ready: take a sharp, pointed knife and separate the flakes of the fish at the thickest part. If the flakes look creamy all the way through, the fish is cooked.

8 When ready, serve with half a lemon on each plate and creamy mashed potatoes sprinkled with chopped chives.

Fish Cakes

*** feeds **4**

You will need:

* 3 slices dry white bread
* 1 tablespoon parsley
* 1 tablespoon chives
* ½ lemon
* 375 g leftover floury mashed potato (see page 51)
* 250 g leftover cooked flaked fish
* 50 g peas, cooked
* 1 large egg
* Salt and pepper

Before you start:

* Get a liquidiser or blender
  large bowl
  chopping board
  chopping knife
  lemon squeezer
  wooden spoon
  small bowl
  fork
  pastry brush
  fish slice.
* Place a sheet of kitchen foil on top of the grill pan grid.
* Preheat the grill for 5–10 minutes to fairly hot.
* Warm 4 plates before serving.

How to...

Put the bread into the liquidiser or blender and blend till you have fine breadcrumbs.

Chop the parsley and the chives finely. Squeeze the juice from the lemon using a lemon squeezer.

Put the potatoes, fish, peas, parsley, chives and lemon juice into the large bowl. Season with salt and pepper and mix well with the wooden spoon. Taste to check if the seasoning is okay.

Break the egg into a small bowl and beat with a fork.

Pour half the beaten egg into the fish mixture and mix in.

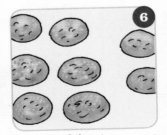

Turn the fish mixture out onto your work surface. Divide into 8 pieces and shape into round cakes. Put 4 cakes onto the foil on the grill pan grid.

Brush their tops and sides using some of the remaining beaten egg. Sprinkle evenly with breadcrumbs.

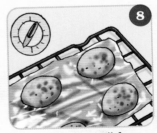

Put under the grill for 4 minutes till lightly browned and crisp on top. Check if they are browning too quickly and if necessary reduce the grill heat.

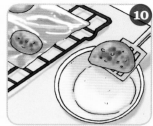

When they are brown and crisp, remove the grill pan from under the grill. Turn each fish cake over with a fish slice, brush the top with the beaten egg and coat with breadcrumbs.

Place them back under the grill for 4 minutes till lightly browned and crisp on top.

Put on a warmed plate and keep hot in a warm place. Grill the other 4 fish cakes. Serve with tomato sauce (see page 52) and a green salad (see page 22) or other green vegetable.

Who is the fishiest nursery rhyme character?

Old King Cole – he was a merry old sole!

Whit dae ye call a lassie with a fish on her heid?

Annette!

Ha! ha! coated fish!

Glebe Street Tips

The fish cakes can also be fried in vegetable oil in a frying pan. Use 2–3 tablespoons oil and heat over a medium heat till hot but not smoking hot. Put in a few breadcrumbs first to test the temperature. They should turn golden brown but not burn. Fry the fish cakes in oil till crisp and golden brown on both sides.

For special fish cakes use some cooked salmon.

Pizza

** **feeds 4**

* Bread dough (see page 98)

You will need:

* Bread dough (see page 98)
* 1 tube of tomato purée
* 3 × 200 g mozzarella cheese
* 1 tablespoon fresh marjoram or oregano or 1 teaspoon dried

Before you start:

* Get a chopping board
  chopping knife
  rolling pin
  scissors.
* Grease or line 2 large baking trays.
* Preheat the oven for 5–10 minutes to Gas 7/220°C.
* Warm a large serving plate before serving.

Some ideas for toppings

* Ham, chopped
* Salami, chopped
* Frankfurters, sliced
* Prawns, shelled
* Anchovies
* Cheddar cheese, grated
* Red, green or yellow peppers, sliced
* Mushrooms, thinly sliced
* Tomatoes, thinly sliced
* Olives, sliced
* Sweetcorn

Some flavouring options

* Oregano, fresh or dried
* Basil leaves, fresh
* Garlic cloves, crushed and chopped
* Olive oil

How to...

Make the dough for bread rolls as shown on page 98. Put it to rise once.

While the dough is rising, gather some of your favourite toppings on a work surface and prepare them. Chop or slice meat and vegetables thinly into small, bite-sized pieces and set aside.

Dust a work surface with flour. When the dough has doubled in size, turn it out on to the floured surface. Knock out the air and knead till smooth.

Divide into 4 pieces. Roll out into pizza rounds or ovals – the size of the pizzas depends on whether you like a thick or thin base.

WAITER! WILL MY PIZZA be Long?

no, madam – it will be roUnd!

5

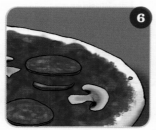

6

7

8

Put onto the baking trays. Spread tomato purée with a knife thinly and evenly over the whole surface of each pizza.

Scatter fillings of your choice evenly over the top in a thin layer.

Finish with thin slices of mozzarella cheese and/or grated cheddar cheese.

Decorate with anchovies, olives or strips of red, green or yellow pepper.

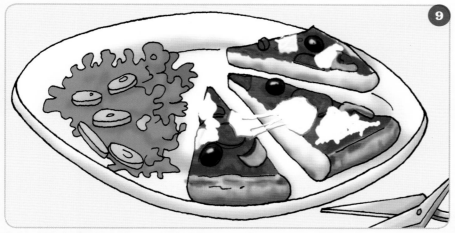

9

Bake for 10–15 minutes till the edges are lightly browned and the top is bubbling. Put onto the serving plate and cut with scissors into wedges. Serve with a green salad (see page 22). Eat immediately.

Do you want your pizza cut into six pieces or twelve?

Six please – I couldna manage twelve

Glebe Street Tips

For a crispy pizza, the top layer should not be too thick.

Moist toppings, such as fresh tomatoes and mushrooms, should be chopped thinly and well spread out or the pizza will be soggy.

Classic Italian pizza fillings are usually very simple: a concentrated tomato base, usually a tomato sauce which has been cooked till it's very dry (you could use the tomato sauce for pasta on page 52 instead of tomato purée), mozzarella cheese and a flavouring ingredient. For a classic Margherita pizza the flavouring is basil and olive oil. There are hundreds of variations so there is lots of scope to experiment.

Dinners

– puddings

Having ane o' the puddin's in this section means the bairns eat fewer sugary sweeties — well, that's the theory, anyway. We dinna hae puddin's every day. We hae oors on a Sunday and on birthdays! And mebbe Saturdays. And if we need cheering up. Or if Granpaw comes roond.

ER, We see GRanpaw VeRy neaR eVeRy single DaY, maw.

Well, anyway, a good rule tae follow is no tae eat any puddin that you havnae made yersel. You appreciate it a' the mair because it's harder work to make it than just buying it, and you'll no eat so many!

— Maw

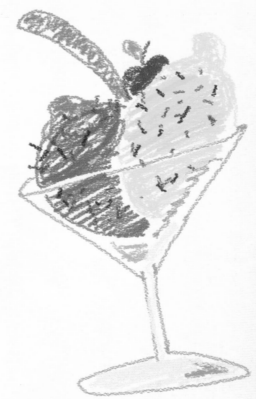

60

Whit's the best thing tae put in tae a pie?

Yer teeth!

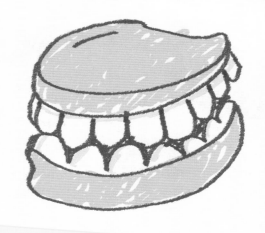

Horace's Food Fact File

WILD BERRIES

Soft Scottish berries would shrivel under the blistering heat of a tropical sun but there's no danger of that happening in Scotland. At one time, wild blaeberries and brambles were picked and sold in the markets. Sometimes travelling people sold them at the back door to housewives who were very pleased to get them. They gathered the small, blue-black mountain blaeberries from the bushes with a special wooden blaeberry 'comb' which had wide prongs to remove the berries.

Brambles were picked from hedgerows. A peak in bramble-picking was reached in Scotland during the thirteen years of wartime rationing (1940–1953) when the luscious black berries were a vital food resource and everyone went brambling. During this time, the isle of Arran was a very popular place to bramble. Hordes of day-trippers arrived in late September, at the height of the bramble season. Brambles were, after all, free for the picking.

JUST look at the state of you – you're covered in jelly and custard!

Yes I'm a trifle messy!

Berry Trifle

**** · feeds **4**

You will need:

* 100 ml boiling water
* 500 ml cold water
* 1 packet strawberry jelly squares (or other flavoured jelly)
* 200 g ripe berries
* 600 ml thick custard (see page 21)
* 300 ml whipping cream
* 1 teaspoon caster sugar

Before you start:

* Get a medium saucepan
  mixing bowl
  electric beater or balloon whisk
  flexible spatula
  1 ½–2 litre glass serving dish
  or
  4 individual dishes.

How to...

What did the raspberry say to the custard at Christmas Time? "'Tis the season to be jelly!"

1 Put 100 ml boiling water into the pan. Break up the jelly squares and add to the water in the pan. Heat for a minute over a low heat and stir to dissolve the jelly.

2 Add 500 ml cold water to the dissolved jelly and pour into the glass serving dish.

3 Keep back a few berries to decorate the top of the trifle and add the rest to the jelly. Leave the jelly to set in the fridge.

4 Make custard (see page 21) and leave to cool.

5 Pour over set jelly. Spread evenly.

6 Put cream and sugar into a bowl and beat till fairly thick but not too stiff. Spread cream evenly over the custard.

7 Scatter the rest of the berries on top of the cream. Serve chilled.

Glebe Street Tips

If you want to skip the jelly you can put 200 g of your favourite soft fruits into a pan with a tablespoon of sugar (if you think they need it) and heat them over a low heat till they just soften and the juices begin to run. Then put a few slices of fresh or stale sponge cake (see page 96) in the base of the serving dish to soak up the fruit juices. Finish in the same way as the berry trifle with custard and cream.

When beating cream, add a teaspoon of sugar and it will thicken faster.

You can crumble a few meringues into the thick cream but only do this just before serving or the meringues will go soggy and lose their crunch.

Baked Rice Pudding

**** **feeds 2-3**

You will need:

* 60 g pudding rice
* 20 g unsalted butter
* 1 level tablespoon caster sugar
* 600 ml whole milk

Before you start:

* Get a wooden spoon small knife spoon and saucer.
* Grease a 1-litre ovenproof dish or pie dish with some butter.
* Preheat the oven for 5–10 minutes to Gas 3 /170°C.

How to...

1 Put the rice and sugar into the dish.

2 Pour in the milk and stir well with the wooden spoon to dissolve the sugar.

3 Cut the butter up into small pieces and add to the rice and milk mixture in the dish.

4 Put the dish into the oven and bake for 30 minutes.

5 Remove the dish from the oven and give it a good stir with the wooden spoon.

6 Put the dish back into the oven and bake for another 30 minutes. Remove and stir the pudding again.

7 Reduce the oven heat to Gas 2/150°C and bake it for another 30–60 minutes. To check if the rice is soft, remove a spoonful, let it cool on a saucer, then taste.

8 Remove from the oven when the rice is soft and the skin on top is lightly browned. It should take about 2 hours. Or bake longer for a thicker rice texture and a darker brown top. Serve hot, or cold.

Glebe Street Tips

Add alternative flavourings at the beginning. Either: a quarter teaspoon grated nutmeg; or a level teaspoon ground cinnamon; or a teaspoon of vanilla extract; or two or three thin strips peeled from a lemon.

Add a tablespoonful of raisins or sultanas with the flavourings at the beginning. Because they add sweetness, you can reduce the amount of sugar given at the beginning of the recipe.

If you don't want a skin on the pudding, cover the dish with kitchen foil while baking.

To make a very rich pudding, replace 100 ml of the milk in the above recipe with double cream.

Cranachan with Berries

✳✳✳✳ **feeds 4**

How to...

You will need:

* 100 g coarse or medium oatmeal
* 4 tablespoons raspberry jam (see page 105)
* 2 tablespoons apple juice
* 400 ml whipping cream
* 1 teaspoon caster or granulated sugar
* 450 g brambles, blaeberries, wild strawberries or other soft fresh fruit
* 1 jar runny heather honey
* Whisky for the grown-ups

Before you start:

* Get a baking tray
  small jug
  mixing bowl
  electric beater or a balloon whisk
  flexible spatula
  3 medium-size serving bowls
  3 serving spoons.
* Preheat the oven for 5–10 minutes to Gas 5/190°C.

1 Put the oatmeal onto the baking tray and spread it out evenly. Put it into the oven for 5–10 minutes to toast it lightly. It should not be browned. Leave to cool.

2 Put the raspberry jam into the small jug. Add the apple juice and mix to make a runny sauce. Sieve if you want to take out the raspberry pips.

3 Put the cream into the mixing bowl and beat with the beater or whisk till it thickens. Do not beat till it is too stiff.

4 Put the cream into one of the serving bowls using the spatula to get all the cream out of the mixing bowl. Put the oatmeal into another bowl. Put the berries into the third bowl.

5 Put all three bowls, the jug of raspberry sauce, the jar of honey and the whisky (if there are grown ups) into the centre of the table with serving spoons.

6 Each person takes their own bowl and adds some cream, followed by some berries, honey and a sprinkle of oatmeal on top.

7 Mix with raspberry sauce for the bairns (whisky for the grown-ups).

Glebe Street Tips

This was an old harvest-home celebration dish in the autumn when the bairns were sent out with bowls to gather ripe brambles from the hedgerows or blaeberries and wild strawberries from the moors. Now there's plenty other soft fruit to buy but there's nothing to beat the flavour of wild fruits — or the fun of hunting for them!

You can vary the flavour of the cream by substituting some crème fraiche, sour cream or natural yogurt. This will give a sharper flavour which you might like as a balance to the other sweet flavours.

Baked Apples

*** feeds **4**

How to...

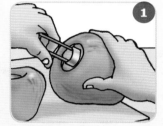

1 Wash the apples and remove their central cores with the apple corer.

2 With the vegetable knife, cut a line around each apple's equator just through the skin to prevent the skin bursting when the apple expands as it heats up.

3 Put the sugar, sultanas or raisins, and cinnamon into the bowl and mix well with the wooden spoon.

4 Place the apples in the baking tray or ovenproof dish and fill their centres with the filling.

5 Divide the butter into four pieces and put one piece on top of each apple. Put water into the base of the tray or dish.

6 Put into the oven and bake for 45–60 minutes. The time it will take depends on the size and variety of the apple. To test if they are soft, pierce the centre of an apple with a thin, sharp knife after 30 minutes.

7 Serve with custard (see page 21).

Glebe Street Tips

Fill the apples with chopped nuts, raisins and runny honey.

Instead of custard serve your baked apples with cream, crème fraiche or your favourite ice cream.

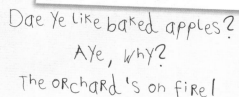

Dae Ye like baked apples?
Aye, why?
The orchard's on fire!

65

Apple Pie

** feeds **4-6**

You will need:

* Sweet shortcrust pastry (see page 22)
* 1 kg tart cooking apples
* 2–3 tablespoons soft brown, or caster, sugar mixed with 1 teaspoon ground cinnamon
* 2–3 tablespoons cold water
* Caster sugar for dredging

Before you start:

* Get a rolling pin vegetable peeler small sharp knife chopping board.
* Grease a 1-litre deep pie dish.
* Preheat oven for 5–10 minutes to Gas 4/180°C.

How to...

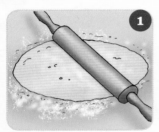

Remove the cling film from the pastry. Sprinkle some flour on a work surface. Sprinkle some flour over the pastry. Dust the rolling pin with flour. Roll out the pastry about 2 cm wider than the pie dish.

Place the pie dish, upside down, on the pastry and cut the pastry round the pie dish edge with a knife, leaving a strip of 2 cm.

Wash and peel the apples. Cut into quarters and remove the cores. Cut in thin slices.

Put the apples into the pie dish in layers with the sugar and cinnamon till piled high above the edge of the pie dish. Sprinkle the cold water over the apples.

Dip the pastry brush in cold water and wet the edge of the pie dish. Place the excess 2 cm strip of pastry round the rim of the pie dish. Press down well.

With the strip firmly in place, dip the pastry brush in cold water and wet round the top of the strip.

Lift the remaining pastry carefully over the rolling pin. Lay down on top of the pie.

Press down the edges to seal. Finish by pinching the edge with the first finger and thumb of both hands or decorate with the back of a fork.

WHiT'S WORSE Than finding a WORM in YOUR aipple?

Finding half a WORM.

Make a small hole in the lid to let the steam escape.

Bake for 40–50 minutes till the apples are soft. Test with a sharp knife through the hole in the lid.

Sprinkle caster sugar over the cooked pie. Serve hot or cold with cream, ice cream or custard (see page 21).

Whit dae musicians hae for dessert?
Flute salad!

Glebe Street Tips

This is a rich, buttery pastry which needs to be kept cool while rolling out and shaping. If the kitchen gets too warm and the pastry becomes too soft to handle, put it back in the fridge till it hardens up again.

You can use a mix of other soft fruits with the apples such as brambles, blackcurrants and blueberries. If you use plums or damsons take the stones out first.

Nutty Oat Crumble Topping: instead of the pastry, rub 100 g butter at room temperature into 150 g plain flour; add 100 g rolled oats, 100 g soft brown sugar and 100 g finely chopped hazelnuts. Pile this mixture on top of the apples in the pie dish and bake as above.

Wee Clootie

* feeds 6-8

You will need:

* 3 tablespoons plain flour for dusting clootie cloth
* 125 g self-raising flour
* 175 g fine white breadcrumbs
* 125 g prepared beef suet or vegetable suet
* 1 teaspoon baking powder
* 2 teaspoons each: ground cinnamon, ground ginger, ground mixed spice
* 175 g sultanas
* 175 g raisins
* 1 cooking apple, peeled and grated
* 1 large carrot, peeled and grated
* 2 tablespoons golden syrup
* 2 tablespoons black treacle
* 2 eggs
* Fresh orange juice if necessary to mix

Before you start:

* Get a large pot with a lid
  small plate or saucer
  piece of thick cotton or linen cloth ('cloot') 55 cm in diameter
  kitchen tongs
  length of strong string
  large mixing bowl
  wooden spoon
  small bowl
  fork
  sieve with flour for dusting cloth.

How to...

1 Fill the large pot half-full of water and bring to the boil. Put the small plate, or saucer, upside down in the bottom of the pot to prevent the dumpling sticking while it is cooking. Add the cloth to the boiling water.

2 Clear a space the size of the cloth on your work surface. Lift it out of the pot with some tongs and spread it out on the work surface.

3 While it's still hot, dust it evenly with a thick layer of flour, over the whole cloth to about 6–8 cms from its edge.

4 Lift up the cloth to shake and spread the flour evenly. There should be quite a thick layer as this makes the 'skin' which is the seal that stops water getting into the dumpling. Shake off the excess.

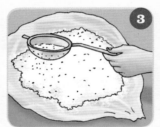

5 To make the dumpling mixture: put self-raising flour, breadcrumbs, suet, baking powder, ground spices, sultanas, raisins, grated apple and carrot into the large mixing bowl. Mix with a wooden spoon. Make a well in the centre.

6 Put the syrup, treacle and eggs into a small bowl and mix well with a fork until the syrup and treacle are dissolved.

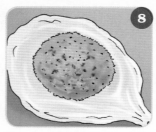

Add to the dry ingredients. Mix by hand to get the right consistency. There should be enough moisture to make a fairly stiff consistency. It should not be too soft, or the dumpling will crack, or too stiff when the dumpling will not rise well. Only add the orange juice if the mixture is very stiff.

Put the mixture into the middle of the floured cloth.

Bring up the sides of the cloth round the dumpling, making sure all the edges are caught up.

Tie round the top of the cloth tightly with string, leaving enough space for the dumpling to expand. Hold up the tied ends and pat the dumpling into a round shape.

Drop into the pot of boiling water. The water should come about halfway up the dumpling. If it is too high it will get into the dumpling and make it soggy at the top.

Tie the ends of the string to the pot handle (or handles) to keep the dumpling upright. Put on the lid.

Leave to simmer over a low heat for about 4 hours, checking the water level every hour and filling up with boiling water if necessary.

To turn the dumpling out: Fill up the sink with cold water. Have ready a mixing bowl large enough to hold the dumpling.

With oven gloves, lift the dumpling out of the pot and into the cold water in the sink. Hold it there for 60 seconds. This releases the 'skin' from the cloth.

Take the dumpling out of the cold water and place in the mixing bowl. Remove the string and open out the cloth.

Whit did The dumplin' say tae The aipple?

Please TURN OVER!

Place a large serving plate on top and turn the bowl over onto the plate. Remove the bowl and peel off the cloth.

Leave the skin to dry off in a warm place.

Hen an' Joe are a big pair o' dumplins

Serve once the skin has dried. Sprinkle on top with some caster sugar. Serve with runny custard (see page 21) or whipped cream.

How dae ye mak' a lemon puff?

Chase it roon' the kitchen.

Glebe Street Tips

Some people like hot dumpling just sprinkled with a little soft brown sugar.

Once you've mastered the Wee Clootie you can double up the recipe to make a Hogmanay Dumpling.

Leftover slices of dumpling are great fried up with bacon and eggs.

High Teas

And no, This is noT When Hen dRinks Tea standing Up!

RECIPES IN THIS SECTION:
***** Open Salad Sandwich
**** Cheesy Beans on Toast
**** Eggy Bread
**** Scrambled Eggs
**** Baked Potato with Fillings

WhiT STARTS wi' "T", ends wi' "T" and is filled wi' "T"?

A TeapoT!

I just love a guid high tea. Real high teas mean ye get dressed up in yer Sunday best, fur coat and a' (fake fur of course!) and get yer man tae treat ye tae high tea at the Station Hotel.

Ye get shown tae a table that already has a big silver cake stand wi' hunners o' iced cakes, currant buns and a' manner o' scones and the like — but ye hae tae eat a steak or a nice bit o' battered fish afore ye get roond tae the cakes. Try tellin' yer bairns for nearly an hour no' tae touch the cakes! Nightmare!

Ye can knock up a simple high tea like the anes ye'll find in this section in the twinkling of an eye. The likes o' beans on toast, and scrambled eggies are great fillers for yer bairns when they come in from school starvin' with 'feed-me-now' faces. And don't forget ye can finish off wi' a wee bit of home baking (hae a keek at the next section).

— Maw

Anither SORT o' high Tea!

Horace's Food Fact File
HIGH, PLAIN AND AFTERNOON TEAS

When the tearoom was introduced to Glasgow in the late 1800s, a 'heigh' tea was a posh treat. A huge three-tiered, silver cake-stand filled the centre of the table. You started on the bottom tier with bread and butter, while scones, pancakes, crumpets and spicy teabreads were one-up. But on the top-tier were the yummy cakes known as 'fancies' which included cakes of all shapes and colours from a pink iced 'French' cake to a sugar-dusted, cream-filled cookie. To go with this was a simple main course, such as scrambled eggs or a cold ham salad. The 'heigh' tea on tearoom menus had been invented to make it different from a 'plain' tea which had no main course. This eventually became known as an 'afternoon' tea because that was when most posh tearooms or hotel restaurants served it.

Meanwhile at home, tea was just tea. It was an easily prepared, sometimes not even a cooked, main course served with bread and butter and sometimes a 'fancy' if you were lucky. This tea was eaten in the early evening if dinner was eaten in the middle of the day. But the great thing about teatime, whatever its name, is that there's always the chance of a 'fancy'.

Why shouldn't you tell an egg a joke?

Because it might CRACK UP!

Open Salad Sandwich

***** feeds 1

You will need:

* 1 large slice of wholewheat or white bread
* Butter for spreading
* 2–3 lettuce leaves
* 50 g leftover cooked chicken
* 1 tablespoon ready-made mayonnaise
* Half a stick of celery
* 3–4 walnut halves
* Small tin of sweetcorn
* Salt
* Paprika
* Small bunch of watercress or wild greens (see page 49)

Before you start:

* Get a serving plate table knife chopping knife chopping board small bowl.

How to...

1 Put the bread on the serving plate and spread with butter.

2 Wash and dry the lettuce leaves and chop into thin ribbons. Pile on top of the bread.

3 Chop the chicken up into bite-sized pieces and put into the bowl.

4 Slice the celery into very thin slices and add to the chicken. Add the walnuts to the chicken and celery, and mix together.

5 Taste a little of the mixture to see if it needs any seasoning. If necessary, season with salt. Put a tablespoon of mayonnaise on top of the lettuce.

6 Pile the chicken mixture on top of the mayonnaise and top with some sweetcorn. Sprinkle over some paprika and serve with a bunch of watercress or wild greens.

What did the mayonnaise say tae the fridge?

Close the door please I'm dressing.

Glebe Street Tips

Instead of chicken, use: a chopped hard-boiled egg; or about two tablespoons drained, tinned tuna; or 2 tablespoons cooked prawns; or 2 tablespoons cooked butter or kidney beans.

Instead of celery and walnuts, use: chopped cucumber, chopped eating apple; or chopped tomato; or red, green or yellow pepper sliced thinly; or half an avocado chopped into bite-sized pieces; or some grated carrot.

Cheesy Beans on Toast

**** feeds **2**

You will need:

* 1 large tin of baked beans
* 75 g cheddar cheese
* 2 large slices bread

Before you start:

* Get a small saucepan
  wooden spoon
  grater
  toaster
  2 serving plates.
* Preheat the grill to fairly hot.

WhiT bean is The maisT inTelligenT?

A human bean!

How to...

1

Put beans into a pan over a low heat and heat up slowly.

2

Grate the cheese and put half into the pan of beans. Mix through.

3

Toast the bread on both sides under the grill or in a toaster. Place a slice of toast on each of the serving plates.

4

Divide beans equally between the two plates and cover with the remaining cheese.

5

Put each plate under the grill briefly to melt the cheese. Serve.

This is high Tea When TheRe's nae chairs!

Glebe Street Tips

Instead of cheese: fry a finely sliced onion and two sausages till crisp and brown and serve on top of the beans on toast.

Instead of toast: bake two potatoes in the oven (see page 78). Split open and fill with either the cheesy beans or beans, sausages and onion.

Eggy Bread

feeds **2**

****

You will need:

* 3 medium eggs
* 1 tablespoon milk
* 2 large slices of bread
* 2 tablespoons sunflower oil
* 1 lemon, halved
* Caster sugar for dusting

Before you start:

* Get a wide shallow dish (for soaking the bread)
  small bowl
  fork
  fish slice or spatula
  large frying pan.
* Warm 2 plates before serving.

How to...

Beat eggs and milk in the small bowl with a fork till thoroughly mixed.

Pour half of the egg mixture into the shallow dish.

Put a slice of bread into the mixture. Leave for a minute till the bread soaks up the egg.

Turn and leave for another minute on the other side. Cut the slice of bread in half or leave whole.

Heat the frying pan over a medium heat and add the oil. To test if the oil is hot enough: drop a little of the egg mixture into the pan – when it sizzles the oil is ready.

Lift the eggy bread with the fish slice and place it in the frying pan.

Fry on both sides till golden brown.

Place on a warmed serving plate. Using the remaining egg mixture cook the second slice of bread in the same way. Serve each helping with half a lemon and a dusting of caster sugar.

 Glebe Street Tips

Instead of lemon and sugar, serve with rashers of fried bacon, sausages, tomatoes or mushrooms.

Instead of plain bread use spiced teabread and dust with a teaspoon of cinnamon mixed with a tablespoon of soft brown sugar.

What dae ye get when ye throw yer toast oot the windae?

A butterfly!

Scrambled Eggs

**** feeds **2**

You will need:

* 4 medium eggs
* 2 tablespoons milk
* Pinch of salt
* Piece of butter the size of a walnut
* 2 slices of bread
* Butter for spreading
* Chopped chives

Before you start:

* Get a small bowl
  fork
  small thick-bottomed saucepan
  wooden spoon
  toaster.
* Warm 2 serving plates.

How to...

1. In the small bowl, beat the eggs into the milk with the fork. Add a pinch of salt.

2. Put 2 slices of bread into the toaster.

3. Heat the saucepan over a very low heat and add the butter.

4. When the butter is melted, add the egg mixture.

5. Stir with a wooden spoon and cook slowly, stirring all the time to keep the cooked egg moving.

6. When the egg has thickened, but is still a bit too wet, remove from the heat but keep stirring – the heat in the saucepan will finish the cooking.

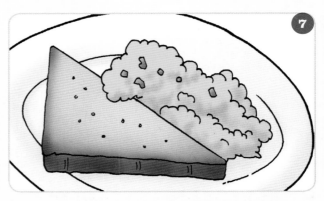

7. Butter the hot toast and serve with the scrambled egg. If you like chives, you can sprinkle chopped chives on top.

Glebe Street Tips

The difficulty with scrambled eggs is managing to cook them till they are just set but not overcooked (when they go rubbery). Removing them from the heat at exactly the right moment is the trick, but always use a thick-bottomed saucepan since it allows you this kind of control.

Add 1–2 tablespoons of cream at the end for extra-creamy eggs.

Add 2–3 tablespoons of grated cheddar at the end for cheesy eggs.

For a special high tea, serve scrambled eggs with smoked salmon and thin slices of brown bread and butter.

Baked Potatoes with Fillings

✳✳✳✳

feeds 2

You will need:

* 2–4 floury baking potatoes (see page 44), washed
* 1 teaspoon vegetable oil for rubbing over potatoes
* Pinch salt
* Nut of butter for the filling
* Salad leaves
* ¼ cucumber
* 2 spring onions or some chives

Before you start:

* Get a chopping board
  sharp knife
  baking tray
* Warm 2 plates
* Preheat the oven for 5–10 minutes to Gas 7/220°C.

How to...

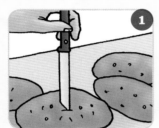
1. Prick the potatoes with a sharp knife in a few places to prevent them bursting as they cook.

2. Put a few drops of oil on each potato and rub all over.

3. Put them onto the baking tray and sprinkle with salt. Bake for about 1–1½ hours, depending on the size of the potatoes.

4. Make a green salad (see page 22). Wash leaves, slice cucumber and spring onion or chives. Divide into two small salad bowls.

5. Check if the potatoes are ready after an hour with a skewer or sharp knife which should go in easily if they are ready.

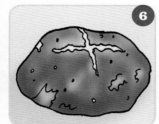
6. Remove the potatoes from the oven. Score with a cross on top. Press sides a little to open up the cross.

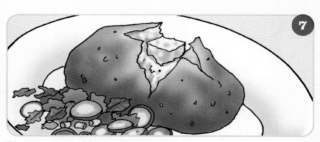
7. Place piece of butter on top. Serve on warm plates with the green salad.

Why was the tattie not taken seriously?

Because it was only half-baked!

Glebe Street Tips

Other fillings for baked potatoes:
* cheesy beans (see page 75)
* grated cheese and chopped spring onions
* cottage cheese and chives with baked tomatoes
* garlic butter
* tuna mayonnaise made with drained, tinned tuna and mayonnaise mixed together
* chicken and sweetcorn mayonnaise made with leftover cooked chicken, sweetcorn and mayonnaise all mixed together.

A Baking Session

This section only needs one word tae get the mooth watterin'... and that word is 'raspberry'. I can mind many happy school holidays in the berry fields pickin' rasps. Ye got a great suntan, a guid laugh wi' yer pals and as many rasps as ye could eat. And ye got paid for the berries ye weighed in (they should've weighed us as well). Happy days indeed! Read on tae find oot aboot raspberry buns — made wi' this wee Scottish berry that's fu' o' natural goodness. And there's also scones, pancakes, shortbread, sponge sandwich and basic yeast dough for rolls and the like, and have I mentioned raspberries? Only jokin'... These are a' things ye mak' in the oven or on a girdle. Now a girdle is like a big flat round piece of metal which is used on top of the cooker but if you don't have one a frying pan will dae fine.

— Maw

80

Horace's Food Fact File

OATCAKES AND SHORTBREAD

When huge black cooking pots used to hang over the open fire, most Scots did their baking on a flat, cast iron plate with a handle which was also hooked onto a chain over the open fire. This was known as a girdle and it could be round or rectangular depending on the shape of the hearth. Travellers carried small girdles, strapped to their saddles, so they could mix up some water and oatmeal to make a quick batch of oatcakes on their camp fire.

This might sound like a very rustic sort of baking but Scots who didn't have an oven, or could not afford to heat one, developed the art of girdle baking to produce some very fine baking specialities. And when their horizons were widened to include refined wheat flour and temperature-controlled ovens they carried on producing very good baking.

Regional and national cakes, breads and biscuits flourished but the most original and successful invention of the Scots bakers was a simple mix of flour, butter and sugar known as shortbread. The Scottish shortbread empire, which has developed around the millions of tons of Scottish shortbread sold all around the world, shows no signs of decline to this day.

Why did the baker work late?

Cos he kneaded the dough

Help keep the kitchen clean — eat oot!

81

Nutty Chocolate Traybake

****

makes 20-24

You will need:

* 200 g digestive biscuits
* 125 g butter
* 140 g nuts (either walnuts, cashew nuts, brazil nuts, almonds, hazel nuts or a mixture of any of the above)
* 150 g dessicated coconut
* 1 × 397 g tin condensed milk
* 200 g bar dark chocolate

Before you start:

* Get a large mixing bowl
  small saucepan
  wooden spoon
  palette knife
  chopping board
  chopping knife
  small bowl
  tin opener.
* Grease or line with greaseproof paper a 25 × 18 cm baking tin.
* Preheat the oven for 5–10 minutes to Gas 3/170°C.

How to...

1 Put the digestive biscuits into the mixing bowl and crumble till they are like fine breadcrumbs.

2 Melt the butter in the saucepan and pour over the biscuit crumbs. Mix well.

3 Pour the mixture into the baking tray. Spread evenly and press well into the tin with a palette knife or the back of a spoon.

4 Chop the nuts finely and mix them with the coconut in the small bowl. Spread the nut mixture evenly on top of the biscuit base.

5 Open the tin of condensed milk and pour evenly over the nuts and coconut.

6 Break up the chocolate bar into squares and scatter evenly over the condensed milk.

7 Bake in the oven for 30–40 minutes till lightly browned at the edges.

8 Remove from the oven and swirl the chocolate evenly over the top with a fork.

mmm ... bRaw!

9

Leave to cool in the tin. It will take 5–6 hours at room temperature for the traybake to harden as the chocolate sets.

10

Cut into squares or fingers.

Why didn't the coconut go to the fair?

Cos it was awfy shy!

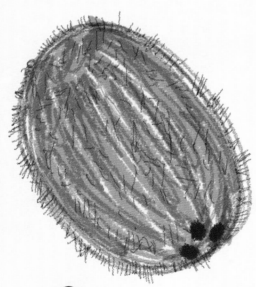

Did you hear about the baker's accident?

He fell off his pie-cycle!

Glebe Street Tips

If the oven is too hot, or the heat in the oven is uneven, the edges may brown too quickly and become much harder than the centre.

This recipe is not as sickly sweet as you might imagine since it also contains coconut, nuts and digestive biscuits.

Jammy Buns

***

makes 14-16

You will need:

* 225 g self-raising flour
* 1 teaspoon baking powder
* 75 g caster sugar
* 75 g butter, cold from the fridge
* 2 medium eggs
* 1-2 tablespoons raspberry jam (see page 105)

Before you start:

* Get a mixing bowl
  sieve
  chopping board
  small knife
  fork
  small bowl
  pastry brush.
* Grease or line with greaseproof paper a 23 × 33 cm baking tray with butter paper.
* Preheat the oven to Gas 7/220°C.

How to...

1 Sift the flour and baking powder into the mixing bowl. Add the sugar.

2 Cut the butter into small pieces, dropping it on top of the flour and sugar.

3 Rub in the butter till it is like fine breadcrumbs (see page 19). Make a well in the centre of the flour mixture.

4 Beat the eggs with the fork in the small bowl.

5 Add about three-quarters of the beaten egg to the flour. Stir with the fork to mix the egg into the flour mixture.

6 Mix till it comes together in a stiffish ball. Use your hands to knead it a little. Add a little more egg if it is not coming together. It should not be too soft. Keep some egg for brushing the buns later.

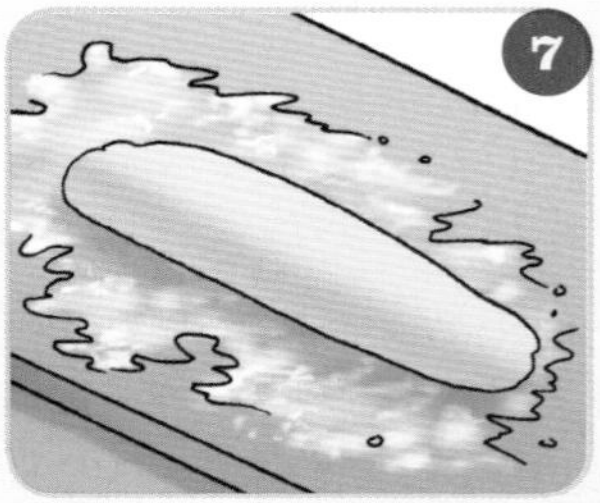

7 Turn the dough out onto a dusted work surface, dust on top with flour, and roll it with your hands into a sausage shape.

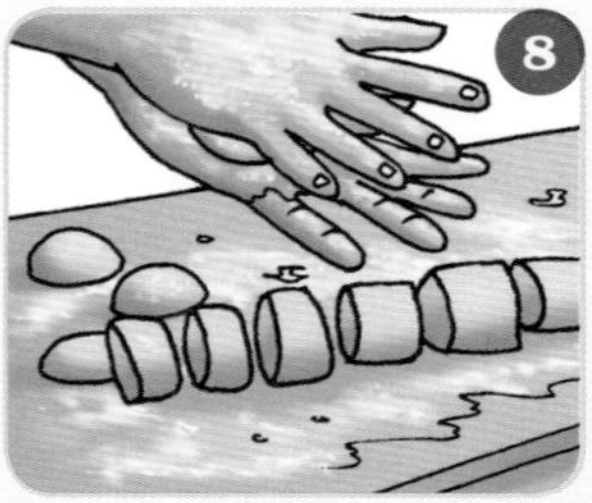

8 Cut into 14–16 pieces. Flour your hands and take each piece into your palm and roll with the other hand into a ball.

Place on the baking tray, leaving a space between each bun to allow them to spread a little during baking. When they are all on the baking tray, press in the middle of each bun to make a deep hollow. Fill with jam.

Brush the sides with left-over beaten egg.
Bake in the oven for 10–20 minutes. Check after 10 minutes. The buns should be risen and lightly browned.

Remove the buns from the oven. Cool on a rack.

There's 11 o' us Broons.

If we had a dozen eggs we could mak'
mair than
$$\begin{array}{r} 14 \\ \times 6 \\ \hline 84 \end{array}$$
jammy buns. That's nearly 8 each!

WHaT does a sLice of TOast WeaR To bed?

Jammies

Glebe Street Tips

It's important to make a deep hollow in the buns so there's room for plenty of jam.

You can fill the centres of the buns with your favourite jam or jelly or with chocolate and nut spread and ground almonds. Start with a little ground almonds in the hole then top up with your favourite chocolate and nut spread. Brush the tops with egg and sprinkle over more ground almonds. For a very chocolatey bun you could omit the almonds and just fill with the chocolate spread.

The jammy buns are also nice sprinkled with dessicated coconut.

Raisin Scones

*** **makes 10-12 small** **...or 6-7 large**

You will need:

* 250 g self-raising flour
* 1 teaspoon baking powder
* 50 g butter
* 1 tablespoon caster sugar
* 2 tablespoons raisins or sultanas
* 1 large egg
* 150 ml milk

Before you start:

* Get a sieve
  large mixing bowl
  small knife
  small bowl
  fork
  rolling pin
  scone cutter
  pastry brush
  clean tea towel
  cooling rack.
* Grease or line with greaseproof paper a 23 × 33 cm baking tray.
* Preheat the oven for 5–10 minutes to Gas 8/230°C.

How to...

1 Sift the flour and baking powder into the large mixing bowl.

2 Cut the butter into small pieces, dropping it on top of the flour.

3 Rub the butter into the flour with your fingertips till the mixture looks like fine breadcrumbs (see page 19).

4 Add the raisins and sugar and mix in. Make a well in the centre of the mixture.

5 Break the egg into the small bowl and add the milk. Beat with the fork.

6 Pour about three quarters of the egg and milk mixture into the flour. Mix with the fork to a fairly soft dough. Add more egg and milk if necessary but keep back a tablespoonful for brushing on top of the scones.

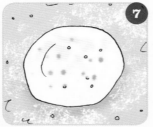

7 Sprinkle flour lightly over your work surface and turn out the scone mixture. Dust on top with some flour and knead a little till smooth.

8 Dust the rolling pin. Roll out the dough to 2 cm thick.

Cut into shapes with the cutter or make into a round and cut into 6 or 8 triangles.

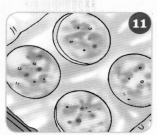

Place the scones on the baking tray and brush with the egg and milk mixture.

Bake for 15–20 minutes till they are risen and browned. Remove the baking tray from the oven. Wrap the scones in the tea towel and cool on the cooling rack.

A balanced diet is a scone in each hand

Serve warm with butter or cream and jam.

I like raisin' scones up tae ma mooth!

Glebe Street Tips

Well-risen, light scones need to be handled lightly. They also need enough liquid to make them rise but not too much or they will spread.

Cream Scones: sift 125 g fine plain flour and 125 g self-raising flour with ½ teaspoon of bicarbonate of soda. Beat together 200 ml of soured cream and an egg. Make a well in the centre of the flour and add 2 tablespoons of vegetable oil and most of the cream and egg mixture. Mix to a fairly soft dough and continue as above.

Cheese Scones: to make cheese scones add 2–4 tablespoons grated cheddar cheese instead of the raisins in the above recipe. Keep some cheese back to put on top of the scones after brushing them with some of the egg and milk mixture.

Scotch Pancakes or Crumpets

*** makes **12-14** pancakes ...or **10** crumpets

You will need:

* 125 g fine plain flour
* 125 g self-raising cake flour
* 1 teaspoon bicarbonate of soda
* 1 tablespoon golden syrup
* 2 medium eggs
* 2 tablespoons sunflower oil
* 250–275 ml buttermilk or fresh milk soured with the juice of a lemon for pancakes (440–450 ml for crumpets)

Before you start:

* Get a girdle or large frying pan
* teaspoon
* some kitchen towel
* sieve
* mixing bowl
* small bowl
* balloon whisk or fork
* measuring jug
* lemon squeezer
* wooden spoon
* ladle or large spoon
* palette knife, spatula or fish slice
* cooling rack
* clean tea towel.

How to...

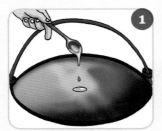
1 Put a teaspoonful of oil on the cold girdle and rub it in with a piece of kitchen roll. Place the girdle on a medium heat and heat it up slowly.

2 Sift the flours and bicarbonate of soda into the mixing bowl using the sieve. Make a well in the centre.

3 Put the syrup, eggs and oil into a small bowl and mix thoroughly with a balloon whisk or a fork.

4 Measure the buttermilk in the jug. (If you are using a lemon to sour fresh milk, squeeze out the juice using a lemon squeezer and put it into the jug first so that the lemon juice is included in the total amount of liquid.)

5 Put the syrup mixture into the well in the centre of the flour and add nearly all of the buttermilk or soured milk. Mix with a wooden spoon to a smooth consistency. Beat with a balloon whisk to remove any lumps.

6 For pancakes: adjust the consistency with more milk to make a thick 'pouring cream' consistency. For crumpets: adjust the consistency with more milk to make a 'thin cream' consistency.

7 To test the heat of the girdle: put a little flour on it and if it is ready the flour should brown lightly. When it's too hot it will begin to smoke – remove from the heat and leave to cool a little.

8 When the girdle is ready, drop spoonfuls of the mixture from the end of the ladle, or spoon, to make them round-shaped, or make your own shapes.

When bubbles begin to appear on the surface, it means the pancakes are almost half-cooked through.

For thick pancakes: turn with a palette knife, spatula or fish slice when at least half the surface has bubbles and the surface is still wet. Cook for a few minutes on the other side till a light golden colour and remove.

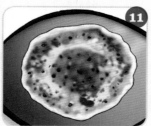

For thin crumpets: wait until the whole surface is covered with burst bubbles and the surface has almost dried out before turning over. This will make a 'lacey' crumpet which is almost 'see-through' when held up to the light.

Wrap the pancakes in a tea towel and put on a rack to keep soft and hot.

When maggie's makin' pancakes she knows they're ready when the smoke alarm goes off

Scotch pancakes are sometimes called drop scones, because you drop them onto the girdle. If you drop them on the flair it's no' the same kind o' thing.

Glebe Street Tips

There are no rules about the thickness, or shape, of pancakes and crumpets – just make them your own favourite size and thickness. For scary monsters, the thinner crumpet mixture is best. Use currants, raisins or sultanas for eyes, noses and teeth.

There are no rules either about how you flavour pancakes, but soaked in lemon juice and dredged with caster sugar is traditional and classic. A stack of huge thick pancakes spread with butter and served with maple syrup and grilled bacon is a favourite American breakfast. A crumpet, spread with butter and syrup, and rolled up tightly and eaten like a stick of rock is a special treat. Whatever you choose: the best are always hot off the girdle.

A note about the ingredients: using buttermilk (or sour milk) with bicarbonate of soda and plain flour gives a special springy-soft texture. But if you combine this mix (as in this recipe) with fine cake self-raising flour you get the safety of its slow-release raising agent, when the air bubbles are not released till the mix is heated. Also a finer cake flour makes a lighter result.

Star Shortbread

*** makes 16

You will need:

* 100 g butter at soft room temperature
* 50 g caster sugar
* 160 g plain soft flour for pastry or cakes

  or
* 135 g plain soft flour plus 25 g rice flour (ground rice)
* Caster sugar for dusting

Before you start:

* Get a mixing bowl
  sieve
  wooden spoon or electric beater
  rolling pin
  star cutters or other fancy cutters
  fork.
* Grease or line with greaseproof paper a 23 × 33 cm baking tray.
* Preheat the oven to Gas 3/170°C.

How to...

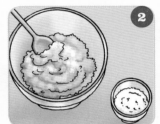

1 Cut butter up into small pieces. Put the butter and sugar into the mixing bowl and beat with the wooden spoon or electric beater till light and creamy.

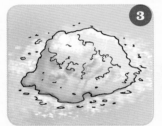

2 Sift in half the flour and beat it into the mixture with a wooden spoon, or electric beater, till it starts to come together. Add the remaining flour.

3 Knead with your hands to work in the flour. When the flour is worked in, dust a work surface with flour and turn out the mixture.

4 Knead lightly till it is a firm but pliable dough. If it is too soft and sticky add some more flour and knead till it is firm but pliable. It should roll out easily without cracking.

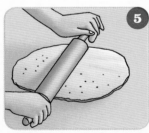

5 Dust rolling pin with flour. Roll out to a depth of about 5 mm for thin shortbread or up to 2 cm for thick shortbread.

6 Cut out shapes with the the star cutters. (Or see Glebe Street Tips for alternatives.)

7 Put onto the greased baking tin. Prick all the way through with a fork to prevent the shortbread rising as it bakes.

8 Bake until an even golden brown. The time will depend on the thickness of the shortbread: 5 mm will take 20–30 minutes. Shortbread should be baked slowly to develop a good flavour and even colour. Better to bake longer and cooler than faster and hotter.

Could we use shortbread tae mak' oor sandwiches?

Cool on a rack and dust with caster sugar.

Where dae biscuits sleep at night?

Under bakin' sheets!

Glebe Street Tips

The 'firm but pliable' texture of the dough is crucial to the finished result. If it's too firm it will be difficult to roll and shape but if it's too pliable it will not hold its shape when baked. Check with Maw to get the texture right.

Sugar-crusted Shortbread Rounds: roll the shortbread mixture into a sausage shape about 5 cm in diameter. Then roll in Demerara or granulated sugar. Put in a cool place to harden. Cut in slices to make a round biscuit.

Moulded Shortbread Shapes: dust a wooden mould with flour, knock out the excess, then press shortbread mix into the mould. Level on top with a rolling pin then knock out carefully against the edge of the work surface holding one hand underneath to catch the shortbread. It will take a bit longer to bake.

Baked in a Tin Shortbread Fingers: this is the easiest baking method. Press the mix into a baking tin and spread it out evenly with a palette knife, before cutting into fingers. The texture with this method is a little less open since shortbread needs room to expand as it bakes.

Gingerbread Man

*** **makes 16**

You will need:

* 125 g butter
* 100 g soft brown sugar
* 3 tablespoons golden syrup
* 1 teaspoon ground ginger
* 1 teaspoon ground cinnamon
* 1 large egg
* 320 g self-raising flour
* 1 tablespoon currants or chocolate chips

Before you start:

* Get a medium-sized saucepan
  small knife
  wooden spoon
  plate
  rolling pin
  gingerbread man/woman cutter or other fancy cutters
  coloured ribbons.
* Grease or line with greaseproof paper 2 × 23 × 33 cm baking trays.
* Preheat the oven for 5–10 minutes to Gas 4/180°C.

How to...

1. Cut the butter into small pieces.

2. Put the pan over a very low heat and add the butter. Stir till the butter just melts. Remove from the heat.

3. Add the sugar, syrup, ginger and cinnamon and mix into the melted butter. Break in the egg and beat well with the wooden spoon.

4. Add the flour and mix with the wooden spoon till it forms a firm pliable dough. Knead with your hands to bring it together into a smooth dough.

5. Put the dough on a plate and leave in the fridge for half an hour.

6. Dust rolling pin with flour. Dust a work surface lightly with flour and roll out the dough to about 3 mm thick.

7. Cut into shapes using the gingerbread man/woman cutters.

8. Put onto the baking trays, leaving space for spreading. Press in currants or chocolate chips for eyes, nose, mouth and buttons. Bake till lightly browned for about 10–20 minutes. Leave to cool on the tray.

I've got a crocodile named Ginger.
Does Ginger bite?
no, but ginger snaps!

9

Tie coloured ribbons round their necks if you want to hang them up on your Christmas tree.

We bite The heids aff The gingerBread men FiRST, Tae piT Them ooT Their misery. EaTin' Them feeT FiRST is jUST cRUel!

Glebe Street Tips

If you don't have a gingerbread-man cutter you can draw your own gingerbread man and/or woman shape on a piece of firm paper or thin cardboard and cut it out. It's best to make the shape as simple as possible (a gingerbread woman could have her arms behind her back and a long skirt). Place the shape on top of the rolled-out dough and cut round it with a sharp knife.

To decorate by painting with coloured water icing: sift a few tablespoons of icing sugar into a bowl and add enough water to make a thin, but not too runny, consistency which can be painted onto the gingerbread with a pastry brush. Make two or three different colours of water icing using food colouring and paint clothing on the gingerbread people. Decorate with small sweeties, chocolate chips, silver balls or fancy cake decorations. Leave to set, tie with ribbons, and hang up as a decoration or on your Christmas tree.

Thin Oatcakes

***

makes 14-16

You will need:

* 150 g medium oatmeal
* 50 g coarse oatmeal
* 50 g plain flour
* 75 ml boiling water
* 40 g butter

Before you start:

* Get a mixing bowl
  measuring jug
  spoon
  fork
  rolling pin
  23 × 33 cm baking tray
  piece of kitchen foil the size of the
  baking tray.
* Preheat the oven to Gas 4/180°C.

How to...

We've never seen cakes like these afore.

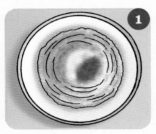

1. Put medium and coarse oatmeal and flour into the bowl. Mix together and make a well in the centre.

2. Put the boiling water into the measuring jug. Chop up and add the butter.

3. Stir with a spoon to dissolve the butter and pour into oatmeal and flour.

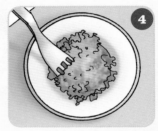

4. Stir with a fork to bring the mixture together.

5. Knead into a firm ball in the bowl.

6. Dust foil and rolling pin with flour. Put the mixture onto the foil and roll it out thinly to about 3 mm thick.

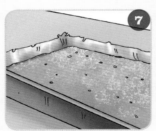

7. Lift carefully into the baking tray and neaten the edges.

8. Cut into squares.

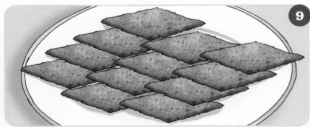

9. Bake for about 30–40 minutes till crisp. Cool on a rack.

Glebe Street Tips

It's important to work quickly while the oatcake mixture is hot. When it cools it's not so easy to roll out thinly.

Shape into two rounds and cut into triangles for traditional oatcakes.

Use cutters to make different shapes.

You can vary the texture of your oatcakes by changing the proportions of the medium and coarse oatmeal. You could also use fine oatmeal and pinhead (which consists of the whole grain cut into two and is very coarse).

Sponge Sandwich

** makes 2 × 20 cm

You will need:

* 4 large eggs (250 ml)
* 250 g self-raising cake flour
* 1 teaspoon baking powder
* 250 g caster sugar
* 250 g butter
* 1 teaspoonful vanilla extract
* 1–2 tablespoons milk
* Jam for filling
* Icing sugar to dust on top

Before you start:

* Get a medium bowl
  measuring jug
  balloon whisk
  sieve
  large mixing bowl
  electric hand beater or electric mixer
  flexible spatula
  skewer or sharp knife
  cooling rack
  fork.
* Grease or line with greaseproof paper 2 × 20 cm round baking tins.
* Put the butter in a warm place till soft but not melted.
* Preheat the oven for 5–10 minutes to Gas 4/180°C.

Twins' Top Tip: This kind of sandwich isnae a piece – dinna get mixed up

How to...

1. Warm the eggs: put into a bowl of hot but not boiling water. Leave for 2 minutes.

2. Take out the eggs and break into the measuring jug. Whisk till thoroughly mixed.

3. Sift the self-raising flour, baking powder and sugar into the mixing bowl and beat with the electric beater for 20 seconds. Make a well in the centre of the flour and sugar mixture.

4. Add the softened butter, most of the eggs and the vanilla and beat for 60 seconds when the mixture should change to a lighter colour and become thick and creamy.

5. Add the remaining eggs and beat for another 30 seconds. The mixture should have a soft dropping consistency. Add some milk if it's too stiff.

6. Put the mixture into the prepared tins. Use the spatula to get all of the mixture out of the bowl and to level the tops.

7. Bake for 40–50 minutes if you are baking two cakes or for 60 minutes if you are baking one large cake.

8. Test with a skewer or a sharp knife to see if the cakes are ready. The skewer or knife should come out clean.

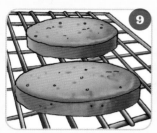

Remove the sponges from their tins and cool on a rack.

Spread jam on the underside of one sponge.

Place the underside of the other sponge on top of the jam and dust the top with sieved icing sugar.

Can ye eat a sponge cake in the bath?

Or make butter icing (see page 21) to fill the centre and spread on top. Decorate with a fork to make a rough surface. Finish with special cake decorations.

This recipe can also make the following:
1 × 23–25 cm round cake
1 × 25 × 18 cm rectangular tray bake tin (20–24 squares)
30–35 fairy cakes.

Glebe Street Tips

This is a quick and easy sponge method. It works best when the eggs and the butter are both very slightly warm. It starts by blending the flour and sharp sugar crystals together which punctures the flour particles and makes the liquid and fat more easily absorbed. Beating in the warm butter and eggs builds up the structure of the cake and also beats in air to give the cake a lighter texture.

In a sponge cake, there must be a perfect balance between the flour and eggs (which give it its structure) and the sugar, butter and liquids (which give it its good taste and moistness).

The 'soft' dropping consistency is important to the finished result. If the mixture is too soft, the cake will probably sink in the middle. If it's too stiff the cake will have a less light and airy texture. Check with Maw to get the texture right.

Because the strength of the raising agent in self-raising flour is not always reliable, since it deteriorates with time, add the extra baking powder to make sure of a good rise.

Chocolate Cake: follow the basic sponge sandwich ingredients but use only 200 g self-raising flour and make up to 250 g with 50 g ground almonds. Beat 40 g cocoa powder into the softened butter. Follow the basic steps for making the sponge sandwich mixture, adding the almonds with the other dry ingredients and the chocolate butter with the eggs, as above.

Lemon Drizzle Cake: bake the sponge sandwich mixture in a 23–25 cm round cake tin or a 25 × 18 cm rectangular tin. Mix the juice of a large lemon with 4 tablespoons of granulated sugar. Spread over the top of the cake when it comes out of the oven and while it is still in the tin. Leave to cool in the tin.

Bread Rolls

* **makes 6 rolls** **...or 1 loaf** **...or 2-4 pizza bases**

You will need:

* 1 packet of quick-action yeast
* 1 teaspoon sugar
* 250 g strong white bread flour
* 150 ml warm water
* 50 ml vegetable oil
* 1 teaspoon salt
* 1 egg
* Seeds (poppy, sunflower, sesame, pumpkin) for toppings

Before you start:

* Get a sieve
  large mixing bowl
  measuring jug
  clingfilm for covering dough in bowl
  small knife
  fork
  small bowl
  pastry brush
  cooling rack.
* Grease or line with greaseproof paper a 23 × 33 cm baking tray (for rolls).
* Preheat oven to Gas 6/200°C.

How to...

1. Sift the flour into the bowl using the sieve.

2. Sprinkle the powdered quick-action yeast directly into the sifted flour. Add the sugar and salt and mix through the flour. Make a well in the centre.

3. Add the warm water and the oil and mix into the flour with the spoon till it comes together into a rough ball. Flour the work surface well.

4. Turn the dough out and, keeping both hands well-floured, knead the dough, pulling and stretching for at least 5 minutes till it becomes a soft elastic dough.

5. Flour the bowl. Return dough to the bowl. Cover with clingfilm and leave to rise in a warm place free from draughts. The temperature should not be hot or the yeast will die.

6. It is ready when it has doubled in size. How long you need to wait depends on the temperature but should not be more than 1 hour. When it has doubled in size, remove the clingfilm. Flour hands.

7. Sprinkle flour well over your work surface and turn out the dough. Keeping your hands well-floured, knock out the air bubbles and knead for a few minutes, so it returns to its original size.

8. Divide into 6 pieces for rolls. Shape rolls into plain rounds or make into fancy shapes: coil, snail, three balls, cottage loaf.

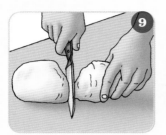

Or make into two small round bun loaves, dust with flour and with a sharp knife score with a cross before the final rising.

Put on the baking tray, cover with cling film and leave in a warm place till they have risen to double their size.

In the small bowl, beat the egg with the fork.

Remove the rolls from the warm place, take off the clingfilm and immediately brush them, quickly and gently, with the beaten egg. Scatter over the seeds. If the rolls get cold they will start to deflate. Put into the oven immediately.

Bake the rolls in the oven for 15–20 minutes till they are golden brown.
Cool on a rack.

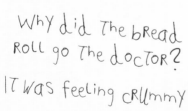

Why did The bREad Roll go The docToR?

IT was feeling cRUmmy

Glebe Street Tips

A 'soft elastic' dough means it should be stretchy and easy to handle when you're kneading it. It's better that it sticks a little to your fingers than it's too stiff. As you knead it, you stretch the 'elastic' gluten in the flour which absorbs more liquid. Developing the gluten at this stage gives a good rise in the finished roll. Check with Maw to get the texture right.

You can use fresh yeast when baking rolls or bread and for the recipe above you would need 15 g. It should be creamed first with a teaspoon of sugar till it turns to liquid. Add this to the dry ingredients when you are adding the oil and water and follow the rest of the recipe above.

Fresh yeast gives more flavour to bread. It's available from specialist shops and you can sometimes get fresh yeast from supermarkets with in-store bakeries – sometimes for free! It's worth asking.

A Bit of Fun

My ain bairns love this section o' the book maist of all and I reckon it'll be the maist thumbed section o' yer book too. This is whaur ye'll find the treats — strawberry milkshake with fresh strawberries and a dod o' ice cream, fresh fruit smoothie wi' yoghurt, hot chocolate wi' cream and marshmallows (I can just picture Daphne's face) snowballs and chocolate sauce. Then there's the sweeties — peppermint creams, marzipan potatoes and tablet. I wonder how many countries in the world make marzipan potatoes for a wee treat!

— Maw

Ally bally, ally bally bee,
Sittin' on yer mammy's knee,
Greetin' for a wee bawbee,
Tae buy some Coulter's Candy.

100

Horace's Food Fact File

TABLET

The Romans were the first to make use of sugar as a medicine, finding its warming qualities a welcome winter cure during their early stay in chilly northern Europe. For coughs and colds they added aniseed, cinnamon or horehound to the boiling sugar mixture. Then it was set and cut into small rectangular 'tablets' of sugar, to be dispensed by doctors. Centuries later, when the rest of Britain decided to change the word for this to 'sugar candy', the Scots carried on using the old word and created their own, unique sweetie tradition of 'taiblet for the bairns'.

ITALIAN ICE CREAM

When destitute Italian peasants set out in the 1860s to walk to Scotland, who could have imagined how popular their new Mediterranean tastes would become in Scotland. Scots enjoyed the rustic flavours in their pasta and pizza traditions, but they also fell in love with their ice cream. At first, this was wheeled through the streets in barrows but later it moved into Italian cafes, which were known as 'Tallys'. And now, despite competition from multinational ice-cream giants, it remains the coolest ice: not pumped full of air into a light frothy nothingness; not made so rich with cream that it loses its clean-tasting milky coolness; just the best Italian ice cream!

The peppermint plant is found throughout Europe. As well as flavouring sweeties and toothpaste, it can be used as a medicine. Drinking peppermint tea is said to help indigestion and chewing a few peppermint leaves may help ease toothache.

Strawberry Milkshake

* * * * *

feeds 2

You will need:

* 250 g fresh strawberries
* 250 ml whole milk
* 4 scoops vanilla ice cream
* 2 strawberries for decoration

Before you start:

* Get a large jug
  hand-held blender
  2 tall glasses
  ice cream scoop.

How to...

1 Wash and remove the stalks from the strawberries. Put the milk into the jug and add strawberries.

2 Save two strawberries for decoration. Blend till smooth with hand-held blender.

3 Pour into 2 glasses.

4 Add 2 scoops of ice cream to each glass.

5 Decorate with some sliced strawberry and serve chilled.

How dae ye mak' a milkshake?

Gie it a fright!

Glebe Street Tips

Flavour variations:

* Use a mix of berries in season with a banana instead of strawberries.
* Make a **Tropical Milkshake** with pineapple, banana and mango.
* For a **Chocolate Milkshake** flavour the milk with drinking chocolate and use chocolate ice cream. Grate some dark chocolate shavings on top.

Fresh Fruit Smooothie

* * * * *

feeds 2

You will need:

* 1 apple
* 1 banana
* 1 orange
* Small bunch seedless grapes
* Handful of berries (without stones)
* 2–3 tablespoonfuls live yogurt
* 2–3 ice cubes

Before you start:

* Get a chopping board
  chopping knife
  lemon squeezer
  colander
  large jug
  hand-held blender
  2 tall glasses.

How to...

1. Wash, quarter and core the apple.

2. Peel the banana and chop.

3. Halve the orange and squeeze out the juice using the lemon squeezer.

4. Wash the grapes and the berries.

5. Put all the fruit, yogurt and ice cubes into a jug and blend till smooth.

6. Pour into the 2 glasses and serve.

What did the ice cream say to the banana? Let's split! Groan.

Glebe Street Tips

Vary the fruit according to the season. Live yogurt has more food value than heat-treated yogurt since it is full of good bacteria.

Hot Chocolate

*****

makes 2

You will need:

* 200 ml whipping cream
* 2 heaped teaspoons sweetened drinking chocolate
  or
* 2 heaped teaspoons chocolate powder and 2 teaspoons sugar
* 2 cups whole milk
* Bag mini-marshmallows

Before you start:

* Get a mixing bowl
  electric beater or balloon whisk
  2 large glasses with a handle
  or
  mugs
  small saucepan
  tablespoon.

How to...

1 Put the cream into the mixing bowl and beat with the beater or whisk till it thickens. Set aside while you make the hot chocolate.

2 Put 1 heaped teaspoon of sweetened drinking chocolate, or 1 heaped teaspoon of chocolate powder and 1 teaspoon of sugar, into each glass.

3 Put the milk into the pan over a medium heat and heat till almost boiling.

4 Take the pan off the heat and pour a little milk over the chocolate powder in each mug and stir to mix in. When it's smooth, add the rest of the milk.

5 Float some of the mini-marshmallows on top of each glass of hot chocolate.

6 Add a tablespoon of the thick cream and some more marshmallows.

7 Finish with a final spoonful of cream and a few more marshmallows on top. Add a dusting of chocolate powder.

Glebe Street Tips

There are convenient, but more expensive, whipped-cream aerosols which can be used instead of freshly whipped cream. However, the cream comes out very light and frothy since it has been pumped full of air and it tastes nothing like real cream.

Raspberry Jam (Uncooked)

You will need:

* 225 g fresh raspberries
* 287 g caster sugar
* ½ lemon
* 60 ml liquid pectin (Certo)

Before you start:

* Get a large measuring jug or a mixing bowl with a spout
  lemon squeezer
  wooden spoon
  4–6 small jam pots with lids.

***** makes 4-6 pots

How to...

Did Ye heaR The STORY aboot The RaSPBeRRy jam?

I'm no' Tellin' Ye – Ye micHT SPRead iT aboot

1. Put the rasps into the jug or bowl.

2. Squeeze the juice out of the ½ lemon, using a lemon squeezer.

3. Add the lemon juice and sugar.

4. Stir to mix until the sugar is dissolved.

5. Leave in a cool place for a few hours or overnight.

6. Stir well again. Add the liquid pectin.

7. Stir well and pour into small pots. Cover with lids (or clingfilm) and store in the fridge where it will keep for 2–3 weeks.

Glebe Street Tips

This uncooked jam will keep for even longer in the freezer.

The amount of natural pectin (setting agent) in fruits and berries varies. Usually the less ripe the fruit the more pectin it will contain. So if the rasps are very ripe this jam may not set to a firm jelly but just thicken to a 'runny' jam consistency.

Whatever its consistency, this jam has all the natural flavour of the fresh fruit since it has not been cooked. It also has all its vitamin C intact, since this is partly destroyed with heat.

105

Ben Lawers Sundae

✳✳✳✳

feeds 4

You will need:

* 200 g fresh cherries
* 100 g dark chocolate
* 100 ml single cream
* 8 scoops vanilla ice cream
* 4 marshmallow snowballs

Before you start:

* Get a small bowl
  small saucepan
  fork
  4 sundae glasses.

How to...

1 Stone the cherries. Leave four cherries whole with stalks for decoration.

2 Break up the chocolate and put into the small bowl over a pan of hot water.

3 Bring the water to a simmer and stir the chocolate with a fork till it melts.

4 Remove from the heat. Add the single cream to the melted chocolate in the bowl.

5 Stir and mix to a smooth sauce.

6 Put 2 scoops of ice cream into each of the 4 sundae glasses. Cover the ice cream with the cherries. Place a snowball on top of the cherries and coat with some of the chocolate sauce.

7 Decorate each sundae with a whole cherry and serve.

Sundae – best day of The week!

Glebe Street Tips

Choose any other seasonal fruits if cherries are not available.

Use a large wine glass if a sundae glass is not available.

Peppermint Creams

***

makes 20-24

You will need:

* 250 g ready-made fondant icing
* 1 teaspoon peppermint flavouring
* 1–2 tablespoons icing sugar
* Green food colouring
* 100 g dark chocolate
* Boiling water

Before you start:

* Get a sieve
  sharp knife
  saucepan
  small bowl
  fork
  cooling rack
  small paper cases for sweets.

How to...

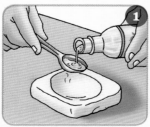

1 Make a well in the middle of the fondant icing and add a teaspoon of peppermint flavouring.

2 Knead into the icing and when thoroughly mixed, taste to check the peppermint flavour. Add more flavouring if necessary.

3 The mixture will be sticky, so add some sieved icing sugar and knead to make it firm and pliable but not sticky.

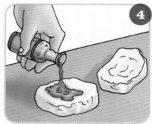

4 Divide into 2 pieces. Pour some green food colouring onto one of the pieces. Work in till the icing is an even green colour.

5 Roll out both pieces of icing into sausage shapes about 2 cm in diameter.

6 Slice off small rounds. Leave these to harden for a couple of hours.

7 Melt the chocolate (see steps 2 and 3 opposite). Dip half of each peppermint cream in the chocolate. Place them on a cooling rack to harden.

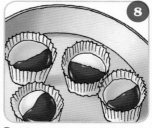

8 Put in paper sweetie cases and store in an airtight tin.

If ye've hae
PEPPERMINT
flavouRing,
dinna use
Toothpaste like
we did...

GROO!

Glebe Street Tips

Other flavourings: use orange or rose flower water and colour the icing orange or rose. Or add ground cinnamon to taste.

Other shapes: roll into thin pencil shapes and dip one half in melted chocolate.

107

Marzipan Sweeties

*** makes **25-30**

You will need:

* 250 g ready-made marzipan, uncoloured
* Some sieved icing sugar for dusting
* Natural food colourings
* Chocolate powder
* Whole cloves

Before you start:

* Get a rolling pin
  sharp knife
  small grater
  small bowl
  small paper cases for sweets.

How to...

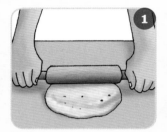

Roll out the marzipan on a work surface dusted with a little icing sugar if necessary.

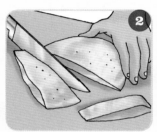

Divide it into 3 or 4 pieces. Keep one piece uncoloured for marzipan potatoes.

To colour the marzipan: take a piece of marzipan and roll it into a ball. Make a well in the centre of the marzipan. Add some food colouring.

Bring in the sides round the colouring and begin to work the colour into the marzipan.

When it is evenly blended in, roll into a ball ready for shaping into sweets.
Colour the remaining pieces of marzipan.

For marzipan fruits: colour some marzipan yellow and shape into lemons; colour some marzipan orange and shape into oranges. Roll on the small grater for a pitted lemon or orange skin texture.

Colour marzipan green and shape into apples. Push a clove into one end of the sweetie fruit as a stalk.

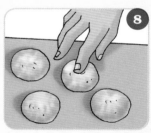

For marzipan potatoes: roll the uncoloured marzipan into small potato shapes.

Dae These conTRiBulTe Tae yer 5-a-day?

Naw!

9 Put some chocolate powder into the small bowl and roll the marzipan potatoes in the chocolate powder.

10 Using your hands, roll out thick 'strings' of different colours of marzipan and use these to make some fancy shapes. See the following pictures to get some ideas.

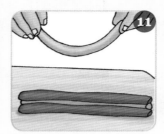

11 Roll out 2 strings of yellow marzipan and 2 strings of red marzipan. Place a red string and a yellow string together side by side then place strings of the opposite colours on top – yellow on top of red and red on top of yellow.

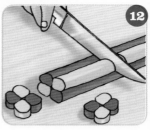

12 Cut off slices of the combined red and yellow marzipan to make small, multicoloured marzipan sweeties.

13 Shape small pieces of red marzipan into hearts.

14 Put all the finished sweeties into paper cases and store in an airtight tin.

What's orange and sounds like a parrot?

A carrot.

Glebe Street Tips

Make your own marzipan: put 250 g ground almonds, 50 g caster sugar and 50 g icing sugar into a bowl and mix together. Beat 1 large egg with 1 teaspoon lemon juice and a few drops of vanilla extract. Make a well in the middle of the almond mix and add the egg. Mix in with a wooden spoon till the mixture comes together. Turn onto a work surface dusted with icing sugar and knead till smooth. Cover in clingfilm and leave to rest before using.

Walnut Tablet

You will need:

* 125 g walnuts
* 200 ml whole milk
* 175 g unsalted butter
* 800 g caster sugar
* 1 × 397 g tin condensed milk

Before you start:

* Get a chopping board
  chopping knife
  a large saucepan with a thick base
  wooden stirring spoon with
  a flat edge
  small cup
  spatula
  vegetable knife.
* Line an 18 × 22 cm baking tin
  with kitchen foil. Cover with a
  layer of clingfilm and place in
  the freezer for a few hours.
* Have more clingfilm ready
  for covering.

We read this wrang an' thought it was a recipe for a table ...

How to...

1 Roughly chop the walnuts.

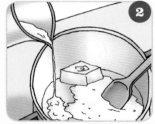

2 Put the milk, butter and sugar into the pan and place over a low heat. Stir while the butter melts to dissolve the sugar. Do not allow the mixture to start boiling.

3 When you think all the sugar is dissolved, take out the wooden spoon and leave it to cool.

4 When it is cool, rub your finger over the spoon to check there are no gritty sugar crystals left.

5 When all the sugar is dissolved, add the condensed milk.

6 Bring the mixture up to a very slow simmer. Stir every few minutes.

7 Start testing to see if the tablet is ready when the mixture begins to turn from light brown to darker brown. This may take 10–15 minutes depending on the heat.

8 To test: fill the small cup with cold water and, using a teaspoon, drop in a small amount of the tablet mixture from the pan. Leave it for a few minutes then roll it between your fingers: when it is ready it should form a soft ball.

Hot sugar!

An adult must help you to make this.

Remove the pan from the heat and place it on a wet cloth to stop it from slipping.

Beat the tablet with the wooden spoon.
As it cools, the mixture changes texture from smooth to 'grainy'.
This will take about 5 minutes.

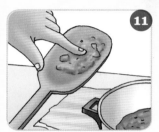

Check the back of the spoon for signs of texture change. The tablet will begin to thicken as it grains. Don't wait too long since it will be difficult to pour if it's too thick.

Add the walnuts or any other flavourings (see Glebe Street Tips below). Pour into the prepared tin.

Level on top with the spatula if necessary. Leave till it is cool.

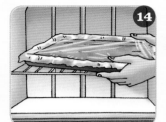

Cover with a layer of clingfilm and put into the freezer for 1 ½ hours.

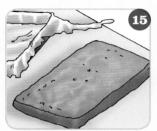

Remove from the freezer, take off the clingfilm and turn the tablet out of the tin onto your work surface. Take off the foil and clingfilm from base. Leave for 30 minutes.

Score the base into 4 with the heel of a vegetable knife about 50 mm deep. Break the tablet into 2 pieces then into 4 pieces.
Score each quarter into 3 strips and break.
Score the strips into small squares and break.

Glebe Street Tips

It's easiest to make tablet in a thick-based saucepan which spreads the heat evenly. An electric hob will also spread the heat more evenly than a gas burner. With gas you will need to stir more often while simmering to avoid burning. Since there is such a high sugar content the tablet mixture will burn very easily.

For a soft fudgy tablet, remove from the heat when the mixture forms a fairly soft ball. For a harder tablet, leave until it forms a slightly firmer soft ball.

Other possible flavourings:

* Ginger – add 50 g chopped preserved ginger.

* Nut and raisin – add 50 g chopped nuts and 50 g raisins.

* Vanilla – add a teaspoon vanilla extract.

* Orange – add 200 ml fresh orange juice instead of the milk.

Horace's Food Fact File — a bibliography

Here are some books to use when foraging in the wild or among the garden weeds. Some are field guides (FG) — small, handy books to carry with you when you're foraging. Others are reference guides (RG) — books to use when you get home to check you have identified the plant correctly, or to find a recipe. If in any doubt — don't eat!

FG: Richard Mabey, Food for Free, Harper Collins new edition 2007 or Collins GEM edition 2004

FG: Fiona Houston and Xa Milne, Seaweed, and Eat It: a family foraging and cooking adventure, Virgin 2008

FG: Vivien Weise, Cooking Weeds, Prospect Books

RG: W Keble Martin, The Concise British Flora in Colour, Sphere 1979

RG: Ray Mears, Wild Food, Hodder and Stoughton 2007

RG: Pamela Michael, Edible Wild Plants and Herbs, Grub Street 2007

RG: Roger Phillips, Wild Food, Pan Books 1983

RG: Miles Irving, The Forager Handbook, Ebury Press 2009

Daphne shoulld listen tae maw an' Auntie Catherine . . . Then she'd know a' aboot whit us bairns like tae eat!

(an' But an' Ben)

FOR BEST FOOD

BEST PANCAKE AWARD

Joe ****

BEST JAMMY BUNS

Daphne ****

Aye — eatin' ye mean

BEST BEN LAWERS SUNDAE AWARD

Maw ****

BEST TABLET AWARD

1st	Granpaw	****
2nd	Maw	***
3rd	Paw	**

BEST HAGGIS AWARD

Auntie Catherine ****

MOST KITCHEN UTENSILS USED IN KITCHEN AWARD

1st	Hen	****
2nd	Joe	***

OVERALL AWARD AND BIG BROON AWARD FOR FOOD:

Maw *****

BEST PANCAKE-THROWING AWARD

1st	Twins	****
2nd	Joe	***
3rd	Maggie	**

MOST MESSY BEN LAWERS SUNDAE EATIN' AWARD

1st	Bairn	****
2nd	Twins	***
3rd	Paw	**

FASTEST EATIN' O' TABLET AWARD

1st	Granpaw	****
2nd	Paw	***
3rd	Twins	**

Granpaw's trick is that it doesnae touch the sides!

MOST KITCHEN UTENSILS USED AN' NO' WASHED UP EFTER AWARD

JOINT 1st PLACE

Joe ****

Granpaw ****

Paw ****

GLEBE STREET FOOD AWARD

AWARD OF MERIT

Wha' says Scotland dishae get many food awards?